KATE SMITH SPEAKS

50 SELECTED ORIGINAL
RADIO SCRIPTS: 1938–1951

BY
RICHARD HAYES

KATE SMITH SPEAKS
50 Selected Original Radio Scripts: 1938–1951
©2013 Richard Hayes

All rights reserved.

No part of this book may be reproduced in any form or by any means, electronic, mechanical, digital, photocopying, or recording, except for in the inclusion of a review, without permission in writing from the publisher.

Published in the USA by:

BearManor Media
P.O. Box 71426
Albany, Georgia 31708
www.BearManorMedia.com

ISBN-10: 1-59393-222-7 (alk. paper)
ISBN-13: 978-1-59393-222-0 (alk. paper)

Edited by Annette Lloyd and Michael Schemaille

Design and Layout: Valerie Thompson

TABLE OF CONTENTS

ABOUT KATE SMITH . . . 1

ABOUT KATE SMITH SPEAKS . . . 5

ABOUT THE COMPILER . . . 9

THE FIFTY KATE SMITH SPEAKS SCRIPTS . . . 11

I: THE DEPRESSION YEARS . . . 13

II: WARTIME . . . 75

III: THE POSTWAR ERA . . . 149

IV: THE KOREAN CONFLICT . . . 229

INDEX . . . 283

KATE SMITH FREE CD OFFER . . . 284

About Kate Smith

Although Kate Smith is remembered as a singer of popular songs, and especially of "God Bless America," she admitted in a 1977 radio interview that she most enjoyed her *Kate Smith Speaks* commentary program on the radio. She said it brought her closest to the listening audience. Surely she also realized the impact it made and the importance of her contribution to shaping public opinion. She was one of the three most-admired American women, the others being actress Helen Hayes and First Lady Eleanor Roosevelt.

Kathryn Elizabeth Smith was born May 1, 1907 in the nation's capital, where she grew up. As a child she loved to sing and dance for any available audience; one might say she was a born entertainer.

Discovered by producer/performer Eddie Dowling while performing as a teenager at the RKO Keith vaudeville theater in Washington, she was given a role as a comic buffoon in his musical *Honeymoon Lane* at the Knickerbocker Theatre in New York. A showstopper from the start to the end of her fifty-year career, she regaled audiences with her fat-girl Charleston dance. Deep down, however, she was hurt that she wasn't taken seriously for her singing ability.

She joined a road company as a black-faced mammy singing "Hallelujah" in Vincent Youmans' *Hit the Deck*. Then she landed a starring role in George White's *Flying High*. Upstaged and ridiculed by Bert Lahr at every performance, Kate's critical acclaim failed to counteract her supreme misery. One August night, Ted Collins, a vice president of the Columbia Phonograph Company, chanced to take in a performance of *Flying High*. Impressed by Kate's singing voice, he made an appointment for her to meet at his office. This resulted in his becoming her personal manager and launching her radio career in 1931. Soon Smith and Collins formed the Kated Company in a 50-50 partnership, maintained for thirty-three years on a handshake.

Kate had a theme song, "When the Moon Comes over the Mountain," with lyrics partly composed by her as a girl. It was her musical signature for nearly fifty years. Her radio greeting was simply, "Hello everybody, this is Kate Smith."

In addition to six fifteen-minute radio broadcasts each week, Kate was appearing on stage at leading theaters. She broke the record at the Palace Theater, staying for eleven weeks.

In 1933 Kate went Hollywood, with a cameo role in the *The Big Broadcast* and starring in her own feature picture, *Hello Everybody!* That fall she went on tour coast-to-coast with a vaudeville ensemble called Kate Smith and her Swanee Revue. That winter she caught a severe throat infection and was advised to go to a cold climate, so she ventured north to find the village of Lake Placid in the Adirondack Mountains. So enamored was she that she bought a house on Buck Island and had it renovated into Camp Sunshine, her summer home for forty years. She broadcast *Kate Smith Speaks* there for eleven summers.

The Kate Smith Hour, her prime-time variety show, began in 1936 and lasted for a decade, sponsored by General Foods. She said, "Being fat and happy, I could always sell food."

On November 10, 1938, the eve of the twentieth anniversary of the armistice that ended the First World War, Kate introduced a song that would change the course of her career forever. It was Irving Berlin's anthem *God Bless America*, his most important composition. She was proud to be called a flag-waver. The script in which she gives the background to the song is included here, as is the one for May 27, 1939, in which she mentions her forthcoming Command Appearance at the White House as guest of the Roosevelts to sing for the King and Queen of England.

Our entry into the second World War resulted in stepped-up activity for Kate and Ted. Collins became an important CBS newsman and Kate added special broadcasts for the military and radio spots for the war effort. She was a key war-bond seller, responsible for the sale of some $600 million worth on her radio marathons.

President Reagan awarded her the Medal of Freedom for these efforts. [See the script for September 21, 1943.]

When Kate's career began to fade in the late forties, Ted Collins decided that she ought to try television. Critics predicted failure because of her weight, but on September 25, 1950, she proved them wrong. *The Kate Smith Hour*, a weekday afternoon variety hour, soon became number one (What else was there to watch except the test pattern?) and remained there for its four-season run. Kate's spontaneity, her expressive face, hearty laugh, warmth, and agility for a heavy person made her a success in the video medium.

Gifted with perfect pitch and the ability to remember a melody upon hearing it played only once or twice, Kate Smith never studied music. A crowning achievement in her career came November 2, 1963, when she gave a concert at Carnegie Hall. Accompanied by a 100-piece orchestra conducted by Skitch Henderson, she could have sung all night. The concert was recorded by RCA and it sold a million copies.

Disaster came in 1964. She fractured an ankle just before opening at Miami's Fontainebleau Hotel in her first night club appearance in many years. Then she suffered a severe throat infection. On May 27, Ted Collins died of a heart attack at Lake Placid. Devastated, Kate went to Palm Beach to stay with a dear friend. While there she slipped in the bathroom, her arm going through the shower door. Hospitalized, she required 152 stitches. Brave and undaunted, she decided to go on with her career.

During the 1960s and 1970s, Kate made numerous guest appearances on the top musical and variety shows. In 1973 she became the unlikely good luck charm for the Philadelphia Flyers hockey team, singing "God Bless America" at key games, which they nearly always won. After they won the Stanley Cup she was the star of the gala parade, as the entire City of Brotherly Love opened its heart to her.

In 1972 Kate made her first appearance at a Nevada nightclub. So successful was her two-week engagement that she returned the next year for three weeks.

She was named Grand Marshal of the 1976 Tournament of Roses Parade in Pasadena, a fitting honor for a beloved patriot of many years. She sang "The Star Spangled Banner" at the Rose Bowl.

That August, she was taken ill with complications from diabetes and remained hospitalized for several weeks. Her recovery was prolonged and never complete. She died in Raleigh, North Carolina, on June 17, 1986, at the age of 79. Her remains lie in a mausoleum at St. Agnes Cemetery at Lake Placid.

About Kate Smith Speaks

Kate Smith Speaks was a daring broadcast venture by Ted Collins, Kate Smith's personal manager and business partner. Inspired by Kate's extraordinary appeal as singer and radio hostess, Collins believed she could also be an influential commentator, especially with women. With CBS President William S. Paley's approval, the initial broadcast went over the airwaves at 3:30 p.m. EST on Monday, April 4, 1938 [script included]. For the first eleven weeks it was an unsponsored (or sustaining) program. After a summer hiatus, the time slot was moved to high noon, where it would remain a fixture for thirteen seasons.

General Foods, Kate's sponsor for the weekly variety hour, assumed sponsorship, the first product advertised being Diamond Crystal Shaker Salt. For the first year the program was broadcast three times a week, on Monday, Wednesday, and Friday. By fall 1939 it assumed Monday-Friday status.

By 1940 *Kate Smith Speaks* was the most listened-to program in daytime radio, an honor it would hold for nearly a decade. So popular was it that CBS insisted it be aired all summer too. Kate and Ted agreed, but only if it could be done from Kate's summer home on Buck Island at Lake Placid. CBS consented and strung the necessary cable.

Bob "Believe it or Not" Ripley described the studio in her guest house as the smallest broadcast studio in the world: a paradox, because Kate must have been the largest entertainer in radio.

Kate Smith Speaks developed a format retained throughout the years. Collins began with "It's high noon in New York and time for Kate Smith. Here she is." Kate would say "Hello, everybody" and read the first item, after which she would turn to Ted and ask, "And now, Ted, what's new?" He would read a few news items, ending with, "And that, at the moment, is what's new." Kate would then say, "And in the news behind the news..." Increasingly, as time passed, Ted entered into informal discussions with Kate. Sometimes they aired friendly disagreements. Frequently they'd get to laughing over some frivolous item, such as a fish story or a new hat style or a banana split eating contest. The audience loved their apparent spontaneity.

Occasionally Kate's voice would quaver with emotion, or she would speak so forcefully and deliberately that the listener just knew she was pointing her finger or shaking her fist. She obviously put her heart and soul into these broadcasts.

Kate's topics ranged from new creations for the housewife to fashion trends to advice about child rearing (though she was single) to how to send mail to GIs overseas. She often recommended wholesome books, plays, or movies. And she frequently aired her views about such topics as treatment of the elderly, underpaid teachers, or juvenile crime. Her closing signature was "Thanks for listenin' and goodbye, folks." During wartime, she added "Remember, if you don't write, you're wrong!"

After more than nine successful seasons on CBS, *Kate Smith Speaks* moved to the Mutual Network on June 23, 1947. (Both the last CBS and the first Mutual broadcasts are included here.) She was unhappy with the censoring of some of her topics. After accepting the 1947 American Brotherhood Arts citation from the National Council of Christian and Jews, she held a press conference. To quote *Time Magazine*, "...the woman who had come to be known as perennially good-tempered slashed out at CBS." She stated, "I don't see why I should let anybody try to tell me how to run my program." Ted stayed out of the fray, commenting, "I think Miss Smith is leaving Columbia because she has a better contract." Her audience turned the dial as suggested and found the new network, remaining loyal to Kate for four more years.

Except for the day of *The Kate Smith Hour*, the broadcasts originated from the living room of Kate's Park Avenue apartment. The daily routine was that Kate would receive and go over the next day's script the night before. Ted would arrive at 11:15 and any alterations would then be made. At 11:45 her cocker spaniel Freckles would be exiled to a bedroom and at 12:00 sharp they'd turn on the mike, which was on the table at which they both sat with their scripts. The program, often described as folksy, was indeed against a homespun backdrop, though always very professional. There was nothing amateurish about either Miss Smith or Mr. Collins.

Kate had a special rapport with her audience. She spoke as if she was with us at the kitchen table while we ate our lunch. Her voice had a timbre and conveyed a sincerity that compelled the listener to pay attention and, occasionally, to respond aloud. She charmed us, you might say. She could talk about an individual or an event "in the news behind the news" that would hold her audience spellbound. Or she would paint a word picture of a country store or the starry sky or the seashore so vividly that in our imaginations we could see it clearly. To be sure, she had a capable staff of writers, but it was her delivery that could turn a routine item into something special.

Kate Smith Speaks spanned a singular period of monumental importance in American history: from peacetime Depression of the late 1930s through the second World War, the post-war recovery years, and into the Korean War of the 1950s. A reading of these fascinating scripts provides insights into the way Americans thought and lived in those days long past: our values, changing conditions on the home front, and the timelessness of many of society's problems.

Ted had every script saved and placed in some forty Morocco-bound volumes for Kate. They reposed in her French provincial bookcase and are now part of the Kate Smith collection in the Howard Gotlieb Special Collections Department of the Mugar Memorial Library of Boston University.

✯ ✯ ✯ ✯ ✯

For more information about Kate Smith, the Kate Smith Commemorative Society, and items available for purchase, please check the website www.katesmith.org.

About the Compiler

RICHARD K. HAYES is a retired high school biology teacher. He has always loved popular music from the swing years as a hobby. His favorite female vocalist is Kate Smith, and his favorite male singer is Pat Boone. His favorite swing band belonged to Glenn Miller.

When a "fan club" for Kate was formed in 1967, he was asked to be the editor of its publications, including two journals per year titled *Our Kate*. When Kate heard this, she called to thank him and tell him about her latest career projects. Now, some 45 years later, Richard serves as archivist for the 200-plus members of the Kate Smith Commemorative Society, which held its 25th annual Kate Smith Festival at Lake Placid in May 2012.

Richard first met Kate Smith on January 7, 1971, when he was invited to New York City to attend the taping of some commercials she was making for Chase & Sanborn. She invited him to her Camp Sunshine, her home at Lake Placid, that summer. At both locations they taped interviews for club members. He returned to the camp in 1974 to record all of her air-check songs from radio broadcasts to tape.

He attended several of her live concerts in the 1970s, always "meeting and eating" with her afterwards. In her declining years he visited her at her Raleigh, NC, home for several birthday parties. Each time he earmarked selected *Kate Smith Speaks* scripts from the bound volumes to photocopy, with this publication in mind.

In the early 1900s he researched and wrote her biography, *When the Moon Came Over the Mountain*, which was published by McFarland. In 2003 he published a coffee table book called *Kate Smith: The*

Early Years (1926–31), from scrapbooks Smith kept, as well as items from Hayes' collection of her memorabilia.

Richard would encourage readers to order the compact disc with the *Kate Smith Speaks* broadcasts. As you read the scripts you can imagine what the voices of Kate and Ted Collins would sound like on the radio.

As Kate would say: Thanks for listenin' and reading.

Kate Smith at age 16 standing in front of the Capitol, 1923.

THE FIFTY KATE SMITH SPEAKS SCRIPTS

A. THE DEPRESSION ERA
1. April 4, 1938
2. April 6, 1938
3. May 2, 1938
4. June 22, 1938
5. October 4, 1938
6. November 10, 1938
7. May 27, 1939
8. June 24, 1940
9. December 10, 1940
10. May 1, 1941

B. WARTIME
11. December 9, 1941
12. May 19, 1942
13. October 6, 1942
14. January 21, 1942
15. September 21, 1943
16. December 24, 1943
17. June 7, 1944 *
18. July 13, 1944
19. August 14, 1944
20. January 1, 1945
21. January 5, 1945
22. January 30, 1945
23. April 13, 1945
24. April 26, 1945
25. April 30, 1945
26. August 14, 1945
27. August 15, 1945

C. THE POSTWAR YEARS
28. June 28, 1946
29. August 28, 1946*
30. December 2, 1946
31. February 24, 1947
32. June 4, 1947
33. June 20, 1947
34. June 23, 1947
35. August 11, 1947*
36. August 26, 1947
37. July 13, 1948*
38. November 4, 1948
39. November 25, 1948
40. December 31, 1948
41. May 6, 1949
42. May 9, 1949

D. THE KOREAN WAR ERA
43. January 2, 1950
44. January 19, 1950
45. February 7, 1950
46. March 31, 1950
47. April 25, 1950
48. July 3, 1950
49. May 1, 1951
50. June 15, 1951

* Broadcast is on the CD

The Smith sisters, Helena and Kathryn, with Helena's automobile: c. 1925.

I
THE DEPRESSION YEARS

1. MONDAY, APRIL 4, 1938. First broadcast. Kate explains the nature of the program, defends the National Anthem.

2. WEDNESDAY, APRIL 6, 1938. Washington, D.C., cherry trees were imported from Japan. Kate reviews *Our Town*.

3. MONDAY, MAY 2, 1938. Kate tells of a work weekend at her Lake Placid summer home, reviews a new novel, "Freeland," and talks about hospitality.

4. WEDNESDAY, JUNE 23, 1938. Some Maine lobsters have been shipped to Camp Sunshine! National Grandmother's Day. Last broadcast of the first season.

5. TUESDAY, OCTOBER 4, 1938. First sponsored broadcast. Kate speaks about her summer and of the importance of radio.

6. THURSDAY, NOVEMBER 10, 1939. Kate gives the background of a new song, "God Bless America," which she is to introduce tonight. She interviews the editor of *Vanity Fair*.

7. SATURDAY, MAY 27, 1939. Last broadcast before summer vacation. Kate tells the history of Memorial Day, mentions her coming appearance at the White House reception for the King and Queen of England next Thursday.

8. MONDAY, JUNE 24, 1940. First broadcast from Kate's island summer home at Lake Placid, done in a converted closet in her guest house.

9. TUESDAY, DECEMBER 10, 1940. Kate has attended her sister Helena's wedding. She has laryngitis, recommends books for Christmas giving.

10. MAY 1, 1941. Not only is today Kate's birthday (she is 34), but she fails to note that it's also the tenth anniversary of her first CBS broadcast.

COMMENTATOR PROGRAM #1 (SUSTAINING) CBS
MONDAY, APRIL 4TH, 1938, 3:30 P.M. TO 3:45 P.M.

TED COLLINS:
Good afternoon. This is Ted Collins presenting Kate Smith in the first of a new series of programs to be heard over these stations at this time each Monday, Wednesday, and Friday.

May we remind you that Kate Smith is undertaking a new role in this series, that of a columnist of the air. Seven years on the air have brought her to this departure. Intimate association with the men and women whose high endeavors and shortcomings, whose laughs and tearful moments make up the tangled pattern of our day, has given her an insight into everyday problems such as few others have been permitted to obtain. It is against this multicolored background that she presents her anecdotes and ideas.

Here she is, Kate Smith!

Kate's first commentator program. As a result of it, she would become one of the most influential women in America and one of the Ten Most Important in the World.

KATE SMITH:
Hello, everybody. Today I'm tryin' somethin' new; that is, somethin' new for me. First of all, I'd like to have it pretty well understood between you and me just what this program is all about.

In your newspapers in the radio listing you'll see me listed as maybe "Kate Smith, columnist." Well, it means just that. Yes, I've got some ideas about things, just as you have. But there's nobody who knows better than I do, that probably your ideas are just as good as mine and maybe lots better in some cases. In other words, I'm not gonna come here three days a week and tell you how you ought to comb your hair, or tell our Secretary of State how to run his business. How you comb you hair is your business, and on the other question I'm just one citizen with one vote; I'm no politician. Now, what am I gonna talk about each Monday, Wednesday and Friday afternoon?

Most of you know I think that I have a regular hour program on this network each Thursday evening. Because I've been on the air for many years, naturally a lot of folks write to me. Now they expect an answer, just the same as they would if they sat down and wrote to a good friend, and because I get more than a million letters each year, I've been a poor correspondent. No one can answer that many letters by mail. It isn't possible. And that's where this program comes in.

This is your program. We're gonna talk over the things that are closest to your hearts, that interest you most deeply, whether it's how to make a lemon-chiffon pie or a discussion on Hindu philosophy. We may, too, from time to time, if you ask for it, discuss some important subjects which affect the nation. When we do, I'll bring you the opinions of experts and I'll give you both sides of every question so that you can draw your own conclusions. I may express an opinion also because I do feel strongly on certain subjects. But it must be understood that they're just my own thoughts and ideas. If you don't agree with them, I won't mind a bit.

Now, so that you'll have a picture of how I went ahead with my plans for these broadcasts, just imagine, for a moment, that you're sitting here with me in a large room with a few chairs and a desk and a couple of telephones. The one item of furniture that you're bound to notice right away is here in front of us; it's a table at least fifteen feet long. On it are dozens of stacks of letters, all neatly piled up. Some of them are beautifully written on the finest of monogrammed stationery; a few are scrawled in pencil on scraps of just any old kind of cheap paper, but we won't worry about how they're written, never mind if one or two words are spelled wrong. They represent something more than just pieces of paper, these thousands of letters. Yes sir, every single one of them is dear, and precious, and important, because each contains the thoughts, ideas, wishes, questions, or dreams of some real person. So ya see, now our long table takes on a new meaning. Our room becomes alive with people from Maine to Texas, from the broad Atlantic to the blue Pacific. They're right here with us, saying what they have on their minds, and they must be heard.

For convenience, we've divided these folks up into separate groups and stacked their letters according to subject. Not, ya understand, because one happens to be from a wealthy society woman and another from a little girl in an orphan home. No siree. Let's just pick up this top letter. It's from a little town in Michigan, and it says: "Dear Kate: Everyone says I have a good singing voice. Will ya please tell me how to get into radio?" Oh, there are lots of those, from all over the country. Now, this next pile here, this is from shut-ins and war veterans, and all those over there in that pile describe people who have shown unusual courage in the face of danger. Here's a stack of correspondence; there's a little letter on top written in a round childish hand. It's got a picture of a duck on it, and yes, this little girl is telling me all about her pets. That's what we call a nice general letter. Under it are hundreds of nice chatty letters.

Then we have a group here which is all about songs that folks like best. The top one is from an elderly couple. They've been married for fifty years, and they say: "Won't you please sing "Silver Threads Among the Gold." Give us more of the old, tried-and-true songs, Kate, the ones that bring back sweet memories. Let other people do the swing songs." Right underneath is a letter signed by a bunch of college students, and what do you suppose they say? "Dear Kate: Don't give us any more lavender-and-old lace songs. Forget the long underwear stuff. How about singing "Dipsy Doodle?" Ya see, all these people crowded at our long table seem to be getting into quite an argument, but we'll get to them later. This next stack of mail contains dozens and dozens of recipes that good cooks have been kind enough to send in. They want me to try out these recipes and see how delicious they are, and I'll get to those, too. In this next bunch, and it's a big one, there are requests for me to appear at certain benefits and donate to certain charities. I often think that word "charity" is a much abused word. Now probably ninety percent of these letters are real, authentic appeals for deserving charities, but a few aren't legitimate charities at all. They're just what is popularly known as "rackets." That's a subject I want to get to one of these days. Then we have a group requesting photographs, and another asking for autographs. Maybe you'll get the idea that most of mail is "request mail," but don't you believe it. Our next group hands out advice. Here's a letter, for instance, that says: "Dear Kate: Why don't you get married? Truly you'll never know the complete joy of living until you have a husband." Now I want to give you a glimpse of another letter in this lot. "Kate," it says, "you don't know how lucky you are, able to get out in the world on your own and follow your career without having to cater to some man. Take my advice and don't marry. I did, and I know." That kinda leaves me wondering (laughs).

Now, let's see...here's another telling all about a stamp collection. What a wonderful thing it is to have a hobby, folks! I don't care what you collect; whether it's ships' models that you build yourself, pictures that you take, or expensive items like rare old books and first editions, it means a whole lot to be able to enjoy yourself without depending on the outside world for entertainment. Some of these days I want to talk about my own particular hobbies: photography, collecting odd and interesting perfume bottles, raising unusual plants in the little box on my window sill...oh, I'm a hobbyist, all right. But right now, let's get on to our next pile of mail.

Over there, on the other side of our table, is the biggest pile of all. This group must be pretty important, some one certain thing at the same time. Maybe we won't know the answer, but we'll try anyhow. The top one is from a man up in New Hampshire, and he says: "Why in the world don't you, a singer, try to do something about the pernicious attempts to change or scrap one of the greatest songs ever written?" There are hundreds of other letters along the same lines. Folks, this is one subject I can talk about, and I feel just the way these people do: mad, clear through! Just the other day, I read in the papers about a group who were all for changing this song. They said it couldn't be sung, that people couldn't remember the words, that the notes were too high, or too low, or too something-or-other. They say it wasn't inspired. Not inspired? Let's travel back through the pages of history for a moment. (PAUSE SLOWLY) It's the year 1814; American is at war; enemy battleships fill the harbor. Below decks on one of those enemy ships, is a young American lawyer. He is a prisoner. All night long, he listens to the roar of the cannon. He stares through the tiny porthole, straining his eyes for a sight of his flag. Finally, the first thin streaks of light spread across the morning sky. And then he sees it: his flag, the American flag, torn, tattered and soiled from the smoke of battle, but still flying defiantly on the breeze. Just imagine the glorious feeling of patriotism, of joy, that must have filled his heart in that moment.

It was a sight he could never forget. It burned into his soul, and because he had to give expression to his love for his flag and his native land, the young man sat down and started to write. That man was Francis Scott Key, and the beautiful song he wrote was our own "Star Spangled Banner." Not inspired, they say? How can anybody dare suggest that? Don't you think he was inspired when he wrote, "Oh say, can you see by the dawn's early light, what so proudly we hailed at the twilight's last gleaming?" I do. They say it can't be sung! None of us had any trouble singin' it in school, did we? We were singin' our own American song and our hearts were bursting with patriotism for our native land-the grandest spot in the whole world today, and the most peaceful, and don't forget that.

It's interesting that Kate championed our National Anthem on the very first program, as she would introduce "God Bless America" in about seven months. When there was a move to make it the national anthem, Kate spoke to Congress in support of "The Star Spangled Banner," using the same arguments she uses here.

Why, only two weeks ago, I attended a hockey game at Madison Square Garden. It was packed to the roof-top. The game was a little late in starting. People were shouting and yelling, throwing bits of paper from the gallery, clapping their hands, and then suddenly the band began playing the "Star Spangled Banner." Why, within ten seconds those sixteen or eighteen thousand noisy, clamoring sports fans were on their feet, eyes front. Scarcely a ripple of movement stirred the air, not one single sound marred the awe-inspiring beauty of our National Anthem. It seemed that a great powerful bond woven by those well-known strains of music brought every man, woman and child in that vast audience closer together. You knew by that silence, that absence of sound or movement among all those thousands of people, that nothing could ever replace the "Star Spangled Banner."

People who want to keep changing the things that must have been the backbone of our country since its early beginnings better stop and think. Let's be proud of the old traditions; let's not toss away the very things that bind us together in love and reverence for our country. There's only one America, and there's only one Star Spangled Banner. There, I've gone ahead and gotten all excited about somethin' on this very first program…and well I might.

But let's get back now to our long table, and all our friends waiting to be heard. They want to discuss so many things: the books they like to read, and their pet hobbies, and the flowers they're planting in their spring gardens. Lots and lots of people are already beginning to think about vacations. Here's a letter from some folks in Connecticut: they want to take a trailer trip. They've got a young baby who's never been on a long journey, and they want to know what sort of equipment to take along, and whether their little girl will be all right on a camping trip of this kind. Perhaps there are some of you folks listenin' in who have taken a trip like this and could tell me how to advise this lady? And here's a letter from a sweet old lady, who asks for the directions for making a knitted afghan. And here's one from two girls who own a little cottage in Maine. Their hobby is…you'll never guess this! They want to build an addition to their house, and they're gonna do it themselves! Isn't that something? They ask me just what sort of an outdoor fireplace I have at my own camp up on a little island in Lake Placid. There are so many things we've got to talk about. And we won't forget all these voices, and these letters. Later on we'll get to all our pet subjects: plays, sports, and most of all, people. We may even get into a discussion of the affairs of State; ya never can tell.

So, join us again on Wednesday at this same time-and send in your questions, your suggestions, and your criticisms, won't ya? They'll all be welcome. Just write to Kate Smith, New York City. Thanks for listenin' and good-bye, folks.

TED COLLINS

Kate Smith, radio's most beloved personality, will be heard again over this network at this same time on Wednesday. Kate will be happy to hear how you like this new series. Write to her, and tune in again on Wednesday at 3:30 p.m., Eastern Standard time. Enjoy her humor, her homely philosophy and her stories about places and people. This is Ted Collins bidding you good afternoon.

Kate holds a script, vintage 1939.

COMMENTATOR PROGRAM #2 (SUSTAINING) CBS
WEDNESDAY, APRIL 6TH, 1938, 3:30 P.M. TO 3:45 P.M.

TED COLLINS:
Good afternoon. This is Ted Collins presenting Kate Smith in the second of a new series of programs to be heard over these stations at this time each Monday, Wednesday, and Friday.

May we remind you that Kate Smith is undertaking a new role in this series, that of a columnist of the air. Seven years on the air has brought her to this departure. Intimate association with the men and women whose high endeavors and shortcomings, whose laughs and tearful moments make up the tangled pattern of our day, has given her an insight into everyday problems such as few others have been permitted to obtain. It is against this multicolored background that she presents her anecdotes and ideas.

Here she is, Kate Smith!

KATE SMITH:
Hello, everybody. The first thing I want to do is thank everyone for sending me telegrams and nice letters after my broadcast last Monday. I hardly need tell you how much they mean to me. A pat on the back is a wonderful thing, and I'm just like everyone else; I like it. I shall try very hard to live up to your good wishes and predictions. Now let's get on with the broadcast.

It was just twenty-six years ago this spring that Mrs. William Howard Taft, then the First Lady of the land, carefully wielded a spade as the first cherry blossom tree was planted beside the Tidal Basin in Washington, just south of the grounds around the Washington Monument and the Lincoln Memorial. The trees, several thousand of them, were sent to the city of Washington as a present from the city of Tokyo, Japan. In the spring, usually in April, the single blossoms burst into bloom—almost overnight, it seems. Then about two weeks later, the double-blossom buds give their beauty to a waiting world. It's a thrilling sight.

I saw them just a few days ago. Of course, there is a great difference between seeing them now and seeing them when I was a kid down home in Washington. Thanks to the Greater National Capital Committee, new thousands hear about and see the blossoms each year, but the same tranquility is there; the same atmosphere which seems to make you want to lower your voice, walk slowly, and perhaps wonder again about the inscrutable wisdom of God in his creation of beauty. Now, my reason for starting our chat today with the cherry blossoms is because a few weeks ago I was approached by a group asking me to join a movement to boycott mentioning the cherry blossoms because they came from Japan. No-o-o-o, not me, because I think that's wrong. I'm an American, and I'll fight for the preservation of American things, but my spirit of fight dies, when it comes face to face with such beauty as that offered in the bursting buds of a cherry tree. Call those cherry trees by any other name and they would be just as beautiful. They are not necessarily Japanese cherry blossoms: they are rather an expression of God's wondrous creation. Would you deny anyone the right to see that beauty? Of course you wouldn't.

Perhaps this is a plea for tolerance. If so, it is a plea for tolerance of beauty, natural beauty, God's beauty. Why, were I to have the opportunity, I would be glad to have growing in the most prominent square in Japan, a vast grove of our own American peach tree blossoms; as beautiful a sight as ever met the human eye! And I would be hurt if there were those so blind to the beauty of God's creations as would want to dig up those American peach trees and toss them to destruction.

I get a lot of letters from youngsters. Here's a letter from a young girl who says her family criticizes her a great deal, and it makes her unhappy because she needs praise more than she does criticism. I agree; we do need praise. But we sometimes need criticism, too. But don't worry too much about it. Just make sure you're right, and go ahead. As an example of what I mean, let me tell ya a little story.

A short time ago I had the Gish Sisters, Lillian and Dorothy, on my Thursday night program. I was honestly thrilled when I talked to them on the air, and I guess I sounded so, because one of the critical magazines of my business spanked me soundly for it. "Kate Smith is saccharine," it said, "Kate Smith gushed like a school girl meeting her first celebrity." That's criticism right from the shoulder. I am saccharine and I do gush. I'm not blasé. Oh, no…life is real to me, and it's vital. People are not just people. All music is not just like all other music. There are all kinds of living, vital people, and they stand for all sorts of vital principles and ideals. They're living and trying and I want to be one of them. That's the way I feel about it, and I don't get myself upset about the criticism.

But let's get back now to our mail…people coming to New York and asking about what shows to see. Well, I can't be the last word on that. I'm not a critic, and I'm not a producer. They've forgotten more about plays than I'll ever know. If I don't like a play for whatever reason, I say nothing, because the man who produced it spent a great deal of time and talent and money on it for some reason, and I'm not qualified to question the reason. You know how it is yourself.

Generally if you see a play you like, you go home and tell the whole family about it. You urge them all to see it; that's what I do, too. If I see a play that really moves me, I want the whole world to know and I usually manage to get that play on my Thursday night show.

That's how it was the night I went to see Jed Harris' production of Thornton Wilder's play "Our Town." Oh, I do want you to see that play! It's really beautiful, and touching and tender. From the moment Frank Craven crosses the empty stage, you know you're in for a rare experience. That's what it is really; an experience, not a play. You forget you're sitting in a theatre seat. You've left it. You're up there on the stage, you're in "Our Town." You're living its life as it unfolds before your eyes.

Miraculously, you see life as an almost complete thing. You see your mother as a young girl; younger than you. You see your father; a struggling bewildered boy. You see yourself enter the scene, confident in your place in the scheme of things, and you see your mother and father make that place for you. And then you grow up, and you see yourself: as a child, a woman, and an old lady, all at once: a complete cycle of life.

I thrilled every time one of the characters in "Our Town" said some simple thing that I'd felt many times in my life, but couldn't express. It's a play that deals with things we feel. Yes, I loved every minute of "Our Town," and I wept all through the last act, at the simple, fragile beauty of an almost perfect piece of work.

Now, I want to talk about a man to whom heroism is a common occurrence; whose accomplishments in the past as a soldier, a pilot, and an explorer have brought him recognition and fame; but whose latest achievement did not make the headlines of the daily papers.

Late last August, as some of you may remember, news went round the world that six Russian flyers were missing in the Arctic about three or four hundred miles from the North Pole. Lost in the icy regions far beyond the last outpost of civilization, there was a possibility that they might be alive: they had six weeks' rations and plenty of ammunition. Vilhjalmur Stefansson, the outstanding living authority on the Arctic thought they might sustain themselves indefinitely on the meat of the polar bear. And when Stefansson was asked to name the best man fitted, by experience and temperament, to go to their rescue, without an instant's hesitation he named Sir Hubert Wilkins. I'm sure his name is familiar to most of you. Danger is his business. He and danger have brushed up against each other since 1910, when he was the first man to get motion pictures from the air of men actually falling in battle along the Balkan front.

He was the first man to take a plane into the Antarctic, and to discover new land from the air. A year later he did the same thing in the North. The following year he flew over the top of the world from Alaska to Spitsbergen. That flight made aviation history.

For repeated acts of bravery, Wilkins was awarded the Military Medal. He has enough decorations for heroism and scientific discoveries to fill an overnight bag. But I doubt whether he's ever paraded any of them for public inspection; he's as modest as a twelve-year-old farmer boy.

But let's get back to that day last August. Sir Hubert, at the time, was all ready to leave on an expedition of his own into the Antarctic. It meant money and publicity for him, but that didn't matter. His work could wait. He started at once for the North. That Wilkins is an Australian, that Herbert Hollick-Kenyon, the pilot who accompanied him, is a Canadian, or that they went on a mission of mercy for Soviet flyers is not important. What is important is that Sir Hubert dropped his own important work and started off at a moment's notice on a dangerous and almost hopeless quest.

The task he undertook was colossal. In the months that followed, he and his companion flew thousands of miles out over the polar ice. Sometimes their compass refused to function. Often, the wings of their plane were heavy with ice. They encountered fogs and blizzards and high winds. Day after day, week after week, month after month, they flew back and forth, scanning the white surface for some sign of the missing men. Thanksgiving came and went. The outside world forgot Wilkins and the newspapers printed few, if any, items about his perilous journeys. But with dogged determination, he carried on.

A few weeks ago, Soviet officials instructed Wilkins to return to civilization. He was unsuccessful; he failed to find the lost Russian flyers. Yet there is, in this new saga of the North, something that we can proudly call SUCCESS, in the fullest sense of the word. These men came through their long ordeal with a brand of courage and persistence that merits the applause of the entire world.

Sir Hubert Wilkins arrived in New York just a few days ago, without fanfare, parades, or confetti. A quiet, unassuming, distinguished gentleman, proving once more the truth of that familiar line: "It isn't life that matters, it's the courage you put into it." Happy landings, Sir Hubert.

A lot of you folks don't get to see the evening newspapers until late at night. Just so you'll be able to keep up with the news, I'll tell you about some of the things that have happened. Then tonight you can read more about them in the evening papers.

Here begins the feature of news highlights, which would later become Ted Collins' segment, and one of his main claims to fame.

Here's a little drama that took place in Chicago's big railway station. It certainly shows that even the most important people are human after all. A distinguished-looking man started to get on the train for San Francisco. Suddenly he began searching his pockets. Then he turned to a friend, who was seeing him off, and said: "I can't find my ticket. Do you think I left it in your automobile?"

The friend started to run to his car to see if he could find the ticket, but no sooner was he halfway across the big station than the distinguished-looking traveler let out a whistle that echoed from one end of the station to the other.

"It's all right," he said. "I found it."

The distinguished-looking man who misplaced his ticket was Herbert Hoover, the former President of the United States.
Just shows, doesn't it, that even Presidents aren't so different from the rest of us.

It's too bad France can't get its troubles cleared up. In Paris all the taxicab drivers are on strike today, and in the metal industries, work is paralyzed, because the workmen are "sitting down." Even the Premier of France is having his troubles. Leon Blum demanded more power over the finances of France. He just squeezed through a vote in the Chamber of Deputies, but they don't think he can get by the Senate.

Everybody says that if France could get straightened out, it would help bring back prosperity all over the world. And we certainly could use it right now.

The people of Buffalo, New York, are happy today. Winter is over at last. The ice has broken up at Lake Erie, and the first steamer of the year has reached port. That means shipping business has begun on the Great Lakes, and may they have a very prosperous year. Incidentally, we're having a real old-fashioned blizzard in New York today.

Now, folks, I see that my time is about up, but I'll be with ya again on Friday. By that time, I'll have had a chance to go through all this mail that's piling up and we'll gather once more around the long table and take up some of the letters in detail. So join us on Friday, at this time, will ya?

Thanks for listenin' and goodbye, folks.

TED COLLINS:

Kate Smith, radio's most beloved personality, will be heard again over this network at this time on Friday. Kate will be happy to hear how you like this new series. Write to her, and tune in again on Friday at 3:30 p.m., Eastern Standard Time. Enjoy her humor, her homely philosophy, and her stories about places and people. This is Ted Collins bidding you good afternoon.

COMMENTATOR PROGRAM #13 (SUSTAINING) CBS
MONDAY, MAY 2ND, 1938, 3:30 P.M. TO 3:45 P.M.

TED COLLINS:
Good afternoon. This is Ted Collins presenting Kate Smith, who comes to you each Monday, Wednesday and Friday over these stations in a new role. She speaks of people and places, and brings you stories gleaned from her rich experience in a colorful life that has few equals.

Here she is, Kate Smith!

This marks the start of Kate's first summer in residence at her beloved Camp Sunshine on Buck Island in Lake Placid, NY. She would spend every summer there for the next forty years. She had purchased one acre of land containing the rundown summer home of a Presbyterian minister, had the house rebuilt from the foundation up, and added two boathouses, two guest cottages, and a wood-storage building. The main house retained the quaint thirties décor throughout, an unpretentious homey retreat entirely consistent with Kate's image.

KATE SMITH:
Hello, everybody. It's nice to be back with you again this afternoon and I hope you had as pleasant a weekend as I did. All day Saturday and Sunday I worked at my little summer camp. We scrubbed paint and cleaned closets and oh, in other words, we let go in a big way on the great American sport of housecleaning. I pulled weeds, put some plants in my garden, and burned brush until my back ached. But it's a grand feeling, after the mental strain of a week in the city, to go to the country and get physically tired. I've come to the conclusion that there's nothing more satisfying in this life than to have a small plot of ground and a

house of your own. It doesn't make much difference whether it's a palatial mansion with broad acres made beautiful by a landscape gardener, or whether like my own it's just a simple little house with the flowers and trees and shrubs sort of growing wild all over the place.

One of the small things that really gave me a thrill at my camp was the hanging of dozens of pictures. Now, ordinarily this is a routine job, but I got a peculiar pleasure from my pictures, because they're old friends who've just been dressed up in smart new clothes. And, being a thrifty soul, I'm proud to tell ya that they cost next to nothing. Briefly, I've been cutting out of home and garden magazines for the past three or four years all the pages of flower prints in color that I came across. and the other day I had a conference with my picture framer and we figured out that they could be mounted on cardboard, shellacked all over, and then put into simple apple-green painted frames, or natural wood frames, so that's what was done. Right now, every one of those little pictures from the magazines is spreading gay color over the walls of my summer home. The simple cottage is a perfect background for the prim, old-fashioned flower prints, and they look so lovely that no one would ever believe they cost less than a dollar apiece. But, I mustn't go rambling along any more about those pictures. You just try them for yourself some time, and see how nice they look.

(PAUSE)

Now I'd like to tell you about a book I took along on the train with me Friday evening. It's a brand new novel coming out this week, called *Free Land*. It was written by Rose Wilder Lane, who was born in a claim shanty built on free land. Of course, as Mrs. Lane says, there never was really any free land. In the Dakotas the settlers insisted that the government only put up a quarter-section of land against $15 and five years of hard work, on a bet that a man couldn't make a living from the land. But Mrs. Lane's father was made of sterner stuff than many of those who journeyed westward with the coming of the railroad, or traveled the weary miles in covered wagons carrying all their worldly goods into the new country. He struggled with crop failures, with work, weather, and sickness, but he won the bet! And Rose Wilder Lane, then a little girl, stored away in her keen, imaginative mind some of the impressions that long years afterward gave her the urge to write this wonderful story of *Free Land*, a splendid contribution to the classics of American frontier life.

It is the simple, touching story of nineteen-year-old David Beaten, son of a well-to-do Minnesota farmer, who started bravely off with his young bride to make good his claim of three hundred acres of wind-swept grassland in Dakota. They were married on Thanksgiving Day. After the ceremony, they all sat down at long white tables, beautiful with shining damask and silver. There were fat brown roasted turkeys, and home-made pies, and great slices of rich, dark fruit-cake. More and more food appeared from the big country kitchen, and the young couple, as they sat laughing and talking and eating the good things set before them, never dreamed that just a few days later they would be lost on the desolate prairie, in a blizzard that lasted for three days. In the years that followed they were to learn more of this country of cyclones, droughts, and snow that isolated them in their sod-house shanty. They fought against poverty, hunger, and misery. They saw their crops laid bare by a single swift-moving storm—the labor of months was undone in the space of a few moments. But they were young and strong and full of God-given hope.

The story is so vividly told, the pages are so deeply furrowed by the spirit of these youthful pioneers, that the strength and courage of David and Mary become a matter of pride to the reader. We tremble with the women when the Indians come; our heart is heavy with frustration when hunger stalks over the frontier; we rejoice when the harrows of rich black earth are broken by the green mist of sprouting wheat. A sweet sense of peace envelops us as we stand with David on his broad acres, breathing deeply of the cool night air and lifting our heads to the millions of bright stars threaded on the dusky velvet blanket of the prairie sky.

This is a story of struggle and toil, of happiness in simple things, of David and Mary and the family they raised. It is a story of battle and conquest, the unfolding of this land which is fertile and beautiful for us now, because into its length and breadth, into its warp and woof, are spun the strength and brawn; the undying courage and spirit of those brave pioneers of another day long gone. Yes, Rose Wilder Lane has written a fine novel in "Free Land." I heartily recommend it.

(PAUSE)

The other day, while eating a solitary luncheon in a small tearoom where the tables were close together, I couldn't help hearing scraps of a conversation between a mother and daughter. "But Mother," the young girl pleaded, "I'll simply have to ask him to the house for dinner after the game."

And her mother answered, with an exasperated note of finality: "We simply can't have him tomorrow. We must put up the living room curtains and get the couch upholstered before we have any more company."

And the girl interrupted: "Oh, we never can have company without a terrible fuss!"

As I sat there, I thought about all the people I know, and the young girl at the next table, and I wondered whether many mothers of the present day aren't jeopardizing the happiness of their children and sacrificing a lot of their own comfort and peace of mind by this needless dread of "company."

Environment plays a pretty important part in character building. Children, especially, are gregarious creatures. The society of others, and the exchanging of ideas, are necessary to their development. They must have friends, and if the little spot which they've learned to regard as home isn't really a home to them, they're going to find their friends outside of its protecting walls. What does it matter if there are a few comforting hollows in the couch where the springs have sagged, or if the chairs are scratched from tiny, restless feet? What difference does it make, really, whether we have a seven-course meal or a good plain hot supper without any fancy fixings? There was a time, not so very many years ago, when folks dropped in for dinner without waiting for a special invitation. A few extra people for a meal didn't throw the old fashioned housewife into a state of nervous collapse. There was always room for one more, and if extra preparations were necessary, the visitors hustled into the kitchen and helped. And who can say that everybody didn't have a grand time at those gatherings?

The custom of "dropping in" on one's friends nowadays seems to be outmoded. It simply isn't done any more. Today, when someone says: "Come and see us," they almost always add: "But be sure to call us up and let us know when to expect you." It seems to me that we're drifting away from the old-fashioned ideas of hospitality, and much of the charm of home making is being lost.

Many of us seem to place entirely too much stress on *keeping up appearances.* In an age of informality and freedom concerning so many other phases of living, the custom of entertaining unexpectedly and informally is becoming a lost art. Why? Why do we fuss and worry about company? Why do we work ourselves into a fever because we're going to entertain our friends?

Naturally, having a house in perfect order and serving a faultless dinner do contribute a great deal to the comfort of the visitor, but the vital question every good hostess should be able to answer in the affirmative is this: "Did my guest have a good time?" That's the only true test of hospitality. If you're charming and gracious and thoroughly at ease, your guest won't even notice whether your silver is sterling or whether the cups and saucers match. Hospitality is more than a matter of table linen, silver, and cookery. It's the art of making your guest feel that you're enjoying his company. It's putting sincerity and truth into the familiar speech: "I'm so glad you came over."

The news today brings the latest move in a legislative battle that has thrilled me to the very core, because the fight is being led by a woman. That she is a personal friend of mine is beside the point. I don't know whether she is right or wrong, but I do know that she took a licking last session of Congress and here she is back again. She stood proud in defeat the last time, and if she loses again, she will still have made the good fight.

The President, as you all know, has asked Congress to pass a bill which, in his words, would put a floor under wages and a ceiling over hours. By that he means that he wants wages to be so low and now lower, and he wants a person to work just so many hours and no more. Because of her long service in the House of Representatives, Mrs. Norton has risen to the chairmanship of the House Labor Committee. Because she is chairman of that committee, she received the job of steering the wage and hour bill through the House.

Last week she met a major defeat when the House Rules Committee—that's the committee that says whether a bill shall be put before the full House—voted eight to six to refuse to let the bill be discussed by the full house. This defeat came, you understand, after Mrs. Norton's long fight to get a bill out of her own committee, a bill she thought had a chance of passage.

Today the news relates that she has made her next move. With the President's backing, she is doing her best with a petition circulated among the House membership to get the bill out of the Rules Committee. If 218 members sign the petition, the Rules Committee can't stop the bill from coming to a vote.

As I said, I know Mrs. Norton, and I know some of the troubles she is having. It's not an easy job she has. First, she had to draw up a bill that would be satisfactory to the various labor elements. That was a job in itself. Next she had to persuade her own committee that the bill was all right. Then she bumped up against the Rules Committee and now she is bucking the entire house.

Right or wrong, I take my hat off to her. More power to you, Mary Norton!

Here's the height of something or other in news from Troy, New York. John Armstrong, a county WPA administrator, became the father of a husky son. He named the boy William Paul Armstrong so that the youngster's initials would be WPA.

The dairy men of the country seem to be pretty excited today about a discovery by William S. Murray of Utica, New York, that milk can be used as an automobile finish. It seems that it solves a milk surplus problem—a milk bath for a car. Well, what was good enough for Anna Held is good enough for my "flivver."

The American Red Cross is holding another convention; the first time a Red Cross Convention has been held west of the Mississippi River in thirty-three years. Three thousand delegates are in attendance. I wish I could be there.

Kate turned 31 on Sunday, May 1, 1938, although press releases gave her age as two years less. Isn't it a woman's prerogative to shave a couple years off her age?

It's almost time now to be on my way, but before I go I want to say "thanks" to all of you who remembered that yesterday was my birthday. Thousands of cards and letters came in, and flowers, candy, handkerchiefs, books, and other gifts kept coming all day Friday and Saturday. Your kindness reminded me once more that my work in radio really isn't work at all; it's play. And please believe me when I say that the tiniest little card was appreciated as much as the orchids, roses and other fine presents. And now, until Wednesday, thanks for listenin', and goodbye folks.

TED COLLINS:

You have been listening to Kate Smith playing a new role in which she speaks of people and places encountered during her varied career. This program is broadcast each Monday, Wednesday and Friday at 3:30 p.m. Eastern Daylight Saving Time. Kate Smith will be heard again on Wednesday at this hour.

This is Ted Collins bidding you good afternoon.

COMMENTATOR PROGRAM #32 (SUSTAINING) CBS WEDNESDAY, JUNE 22, 1938—3:30 P.M. TO 3:45 P.M.

TED COLLINS:

Good Afternoon. This is Ted Collins. (HESITATE) It has been my pleasure and privilege three times each week for the past few months to present Kate Smith to you as she undertook a new kind of broadcast for her, a commentary on life and the news of the day. Now vacation time is here, and Kate is looking forward to a long rest in preparation for the fall season of broadcasting. So it is with a combination of both regret and pleasure that I introduce her for the last time until then; regretful because we have enjoyed these afternoon chats, pleasurable because of anticipation of vacation enjoyment. I would like to step out of character just a moment to tell Kate that I think her new effort has been a real success. Audience, for the last time until fall may I say, HERE SHE IS, KATE SMITH!

KATE SMITH:

Thank You very much, Ted, and hello, everybody! Before we get started with our program, I want to take just a minute to express my thanks and appreciation to some radio friends of mine up in the state of Maine. I have just been handed a lovely letter telling me that they're sending me a big crate of lobsters just as soon as I arrive at my summer home. You know, this is really a remarkable coincidence, because just last night I was thinking that while I am up in the mountains I wouldn't be able to get much fresh seafood. Then along came this letter, and with it were a lot of good old-fashioned New England lobster recipes. I can't think of anything more delicious than state of Maine lobsters, fresh from the deep, cold waters of the North Atlantic, whether you broil them, or make them into a lobster stew, or just drop them in water and boil them. Anyway you cook 'em, they're grand, and I'm looking forward to that shipment.

And now, let's see what's in the news today...

Good news, really good news, ran riot all over the wires today when our Public Works Administration opened the New Deal's spending drive for recovery. The President had hardly finished signing his name to the great bill when the WPA began to announce allocations. New schools, new bridges, amphitheatres, new roads, new everything in all parts of the country will be built, and according to the WPA about six hundred million dollars will be on the way to cities and towns in the United States for work before the end of this week. Ours is a rich country and it seems fitting that we should use some of those riches to tide us over when things are slow. So, maybe our present cloud has a silver lining. A banker last night bet me a dollar that next Christmas will be the most prosperous we've ever had. Let's hope he wins that bet!

Everywhere I go I hear folks mention the marvelous comeback try Mrs. Helen Wills Moody is making at tennis. The latest news is that she has won her first match at Wimbledon for the Women's All England Singles Tennis Title. She defeated Mrs. Nellie Hopman. Good luck, Helen!

Well, I see there's one place on earth where it isn't at all good to whistle while you work...if you whistle the wrong song, and that's in Germany. Fritz Boettcher, a 37-year-old ditch digger found that out when he whaled away with his shovel whistling the Russian national anthem all the while.

A snooper somewhere around recognized the tune and Fritz wound up in jail with a six-week sentence. Snow White's advice is not so good here!

It looks like the big fight will go on all O.K. The weather bureau promises nothing worse than an occasional light shower for tonight when Heavyweight Champion Joe Louis and the German challenger Max Schmeling enter the ring to settle their little difference over who is the better man. Mike Jacobs, the matchmaker, says the fight will go on unless a real heavy rain develops. Well, may the better man win.

Thirty five energetic grandmothers got together last night and launched a campaign to make the world grandmother-conscious. According to the president of the new club, called National Grandmothers, the world has grandmothers all wrong. Mrs. Marie K. Brown said that only mistaken persons think that grandmothers sit around looking like Whistler's mother or just bake ginger bread cookies for their grandchildren.

Equally wrong is the picture of a streamlined grandmother with bobbed hair and smoking a cigarette, said the leader of the grandmother's club. The real tasks facing grandmothers lie in other directions. And as soon as the elderly women get around to it, they'll embark on a program of:

1. PERPETUATING PEACE AND LIBERTY FOR THEIR GRANDCHILDREN.
2. IMPROVE RADIO PROGRAMS.
3. CLEAN UP THE MOVIES.
4. PROMOTE BETTER CHILDREN'S LITERATURE.
5. ENCOURAGE ESTABLISHMENT OF MORE RECREATION FACILITIES.
6. STUDY CHILDREN'S DISEASES.

But the real problem ahead is to "glorify" Grandmothers, says the club leader. And from that we suspect that the grandmothers are being organized by some clever publicity man, because plans for glorifying grandmothers center around proclaiming the first Sunday in October as Grandmother's Day. "We believe national grandmother's day should be in October," said the club president, "because grandmothers are in the October of their lives."

Well, now, America has a mother's day, a father's day and a grandmother's day. Perhaps it might be a good idea to have a grandpa's day next. What do you think?

Nearly 150,000 Roman Catholics, it was estimated today, will attend the opening Mass tomorrow of the National Eucharistic Congress in Quebec, Canada. Trains, buses, automobiles and steamers poured a steady stream of delegates into the flag-bedecked city and approximately 100,000 persons were expected at the official civic reception at the Armory tonight.

A mass at the huge repository in Battlefields Park tomorrow morning will open the five-day religious observances. A pontifical Mass on the Plains of Abraham on Sunday will be the highlight of the Congress, after which Pope Pius will address the throng by radio from his summer palace at Castel Gandolfo, Italy.

Here is a piece of important news from Tallahassee, Florida. It has just been announced there that Governor Fred P. Cone and the Florida State Pardon Board have agreed to hear a plea for commutation of the death sentence imposed on Franklin Pierce McCall, the kidnapper and killer of little Jimmy Cash. The bulletin doesn't say when the hearing will be held, but it is assumed that it will be almost immediately.

Well, folks, this afternoon marks the last of this series of talks until I get back to New York in the fall. To tell you I'm sorry just doesn't half express how I feel. It seems strange to think that I won't be here as usual on Friday, that I won't be checking up on the last-minute news, and chatting about all the things that I usually make little notes about and mention to you on these programs. I'm going to miss it.

Ya know, when Ted Collins and the Columbia Broadcasting officials asked me to start this new afternoon series, I wasn't at all sure how it would be received. You, my radio friends, knew me only as a singer. That's been my main job on the air for several years, so when it was suggested that I go on the air three times weekly without any songs or any music, there was a little cloud of doubt in my mind. I'd done a great deal of talking on my evening shows, like introducing celebrities and having interviews with various people, and sending you a little spoken message now and then, but this series was different; it was new. I wanted so terribly to have you like me, and I didn't want anyone to get the impression that I was one of those strong-minded women who thought she knew it all and wanted to tell the world and everybody in it how to run its business. But there were many, many things I wanted to cover, so many important subjects of special interest to women, so I agreed to go ahead with the programs.

Each Monday, Wednesday and Friday, I've brought you the latest news of the day, and in addition, I've tried to talk with you about the little intimate, homey subjects which, according to your letters, so many of you like. We've talked about hobbies, and vacations, and American cookery, and June brides. We've discussed fashions, and gardens, and new ways of framing pictures. Every now and then I've told you about the books I've liked, and speaking of books, I feel very proud, because both "The Yearling" and "Free Land," which I recommended very highly, are now best-sellers. We've discussed some of our favorite American authors, such as Kathleen Norris, the novelist, and Mrs. Grace Crowell, who has written such lovely poetry. We've talked about motion pictures.

Then, for those of you who don't travel about the country so much, I've spoken of people and places which might interest you. We journeyed to the outboard motor races, and to the faraway island of Nantucket. We've gone on little jaunts in the less well-known districts of this big city of New York. One day we took a long, leisurely ride in one of those old-fashioned horse-drawn Victorians through Central Park. One day we went to the Botanical Gardens , and we went to the circus, too, and through the vast United Press Building to see just how the latest news comes through.

We've done so many, many things together on these programs, and I've tried my best to paint colorful pictures, and bring to your mind the little human interest angles that make life so fascinating. But along with all these, we've talked over some might important subjects. I've urged industrial leaders to give consideration to the discrimination against people over forty who are able and willing to work, but who have seen youth take their places in factories and offices. I've objected to this silly idea of changing the tune of our good old Star Spangled Banner. I've spoken of the loyalty and reverence we owe to our flag and to our country. I've brought you stories of the good that is being done by our G-men, by the Voluntary Life Saving Corps, by our great American Red Cross. We've discussed mothers and the love we bear for them. We've talked about the great women of history and down to the present day. And over and over again, I've spoken of the ghastly and cruel results of war, and have expressed my faith and hope that some day the whole world would realize the stupidity and futility of destroying life and property.

All through these many weeks, with your letters and your words of encouragement and praise, you've helped me. You've sent along your suggestions and your ideas. You haven't always agreed with my opinions, but when you did disagree, you sent constructive criticisms that have helped me more than you realize, and I want to express to you now my deep thanks, my heartfelt appreciation for all you've done. These programs have been successful; so much so, in fact, that I've been asked to continue in the fall what was first started as an experiment. And that success, like any success that has come to me, is due to you, my radio friends.

My dearest dreams have been realized in these afternoon chats. I've learned a lot, and still have much to learn. Maybe you who have listened have gained a little information that is of value; I hope so. Anyhow I feel we're all a little bit better acquainted.

Yes, it's been very wonderful, very sweet, to have had this chance to extend my hand in friendliness across the miles to you. This summer I'm going to be working on my book, which tells the story of my life so far on the stage and in radio, which will contain all the helpful suggestions and the bits of philosophy I've picked up through the years which may be of interest. I'm writing about home-making, and sports, and diet, and exercise. I've got some very special recipes that will go into that book. It's a big job, but it's fun, too. So, even though I'll be off the air, I'll be thinking of you all and trying to figure out just the things which you'll like the best to hear about or read about. And now, once more I look up at that old clock here in the studio and I see it's almost time for me to be on my way.

I hope that each and every one of you will have just the loveliest summer you've ever had. I'll be with you all again in the fall. Until then, with all my heart, thanks for listenin' and goodbye, folks.

TED COLLINS:
So ends the final program of Kate Smith's new series of broadcasts to which you have been listening each Monday, Wednesday and Friday for the past few months. Vacation pleasures call, and she will not return to the air until the summer is over. As Kate has said goodbye to you, may I also. I, too, have enjoyed being with Kate on these programs, and I have enjoyed, as your letters say you have, her philosophy and her viewpoints on life and the news of the day. Next fall we shall again take up our air visits where we leave off today. Until that time, this is Ted Collins, bidding you good afternoon.

KATE SMITH DIAMOND CRYSTAL PROGRAM #1 (CBS)
TUESDAY, OCT 4, 1938

The first sponsored broadcast, and the first at high noon, where it would remain for 13 years.

TED COLLINS:

It's high noon, and time for Kate Smith in the first of a series of talks about the things you like to hear. Kate is brought to you by the makers of her favorite salt, Diamond Crystal Shaker Salt in the round, red package with the picture of the Shaker Girl; the salt that makes good food taste better. Kate Smith comes to you at noon every Tuesday, Thursday, and Saturday with a quarter-hour of news, comment, and stories about people who may live around the corner from you. Here she is, Kate Smith!

KATE SMITH:

Thanks, Ted, and hello, everybody! It's grand getting back to this microphone after being away all summer. I've missed our little talks and I'm hoping that some of you old friends are saying to yourselves right now: "Why, Kate's back!" Yes, here I am, happy and healthy, and filled with plans to bring you all sorts of interesting features on these programs. I've been away in the mountains, you know, getting a good rest and making my mind clear and fresh for a season of broadcasting. I kept pretty busy, though, in spite of myself. It wasn't all swimming and fishing and sitting in the sun. I put a brand new model kitchen into my camp at Lake Placid, and almost every day I took time out to work on my book. Writing has always been one of my secret passions, and when I actually see that book in print next week, well, I'm going to be pretty thrilled.

Kate's autobiography, Living in a Great Big Way, *was published later that month.*

I spent a lot of time in the woods, too, where it's lonesome and quiet and peaceful. It seems, somehow, that I can think more clearly when I'm all by myself among the tall trees. You sort of get closer to God when you're in the heart of the hills, breathing the clean fresh air filled with the scent of the pines. I used to lie out there staring at the blue sky overhead. I did a lot of thinking: about singing, about the things I wanted to get into my book, and, maybe more than anything else, about these little talks I'm going to have with you all winter. Above everything else, I think these talks are closest to my heart, and I hope they'll be close to your hearts, too. But I'll tell you more about what we're trying to do on these programs in a few minutes. Right now, I want to tell you about a girl I know; just an average young American girl with keen bright eyes that look straight into your own. Her name is Jeannie. I met her recently when she was on her way to one of our eastern colleges. We got to talking about all sorts of things: clothes, politics, careers, the changes of the younger generation getting along in this mixed-up world of today, and finally I asked: "Jeannie, honestly, what do you want most in life?" her laughing brown eyes grew thoughtful. "I want to make good in college. After that, a job, and then, maybe, marriage and children of my own." Most girls want all these things.

"But what, most of all?" I insisted, and after a moment this young, eager, modern little girl came back at me.

"More than anything else in the world," she said firmly, "I want the ability to see and think straight, and the courage to face whatever life holds."

Now, a whole lot has been said lately about what's going to happen to the youth of this country, and the pessimistic attitude of some of the younger generation about present economic conditions. But if Jeannie represents the average college student, and I think she does, I should say that the one biggest asset for the future of our country lies in the straight forward fearless attitude of these intelligent youngsters who will carry on in the years to come. They've got awareness, understanding, and courage. Those three qualities are within the reach of all of us, if we just stop and think. If we possess that greatest of all gifts, COURAGE, there isn't any circumstance, any condition, that we need fear. And having courage doesn't mean just sitting back, Pollyanna fashion, hoping for the best. No. It means facing life intelligently, doing our utmost, each in our own small way, increasing our knowledge, trying to better ourselves. If, for instance, we take an interest in the politics of our country, finding out all we can on the subject, know why we're voting as we do, being honest with ourselves, and those around us, using our brains instead of depending upon the brains of other people. Tackling life with determination to make the best we can out of it, that's courage. It's the stuff that built this country of ours, and regardless of present conditions, or propaganda, or "isms," it's the stuff that's going to keep us going. Courage, and that ability Jeannie talks about: to see and think straight.

Yes sir, if we women have these qualities, we're going in the right direction. Whether we're applying the doctrine to some complex, intricate problem, or just going about the simple business of baking a chocolate layer cake, or cooking a little dinner for family.

(FIRST COMMERCIAL)

Not so many years ago, the sightless were accepted as a responsibility. Everybody felt that those poor, unfortunates, called "the blind" were to be pitied and taken care of, because they could be of no real use in the world as far as earning their living was concerned. But, during the last few years blind people everywhere have been proving that they can and will turn the senses they have left toward becoming useful members of society. It's heartening to hear about the accomplishments of a man who, although handicapped by the complete loss of his eyesight nine years ago, did not sit back with folded hands. His name is Berthold Ordner. Before he was stricken with blindness he worked as a banker. When he could no longer carry on in that job, he turned to art, and he found not only an escape, but a new life. After trying many mediums, he figured out a new method of forming figures by twisting and looping wire over a frame. By using different types and sizes of wire, and by the sensitive touch developed in his fingertips, he has been able to turn out wire creations that are not only beautiful, but which are unique in style. In 1937, the Newhouse Galleries exhibited Mr. Ordner's work, and art critics were amazed at the feeling expressed in these wire figures.

Mr. Ordner has a leaning toward the modeling of prehistoric animals. He recently sold to one of the large oil refining companies a figure of a dinosaur to add to their collection. It is 26 inches long and about a foot high. In every little detail it's accurate and true to form. And when you think that this "wire-plastic" as Mr. Ordner calls it, was made with no other tools than pincers and wire cutters, that he could not see his finished work and that it is acceptable artistically and commercially, why you just have to take off your hat to Mr. Ordner and say three cheers!

(SECOND COMMERCIAL)

I wonder if you folks listenin' in right now realize just how important radio is. It was brought home most forcibly to me last week, when everybody was listening, waiting in agonized tension for the news from Europe. The destiny of perhaps the entire civilized world was being decided, the peace and security of millions of homes was being threatened, and here in America, we did not have to depend upon rumors or delayed reports. We sat in our living rooms, safe and secure, and radio brought us not only the actual voices of our correspondents abroad by means of short wave, but also followed their reports with a clear interpretation of what they told us. It was reported that in certain countries various devices were used to fog and confuse the talks coming over so that local stations in Europe could not get information from one another.

But principled agitators held no sway over American radio! Radio officials, sponsors, technicians, announcers—everybody here forgot schedules, forgot time, and worked unceasingly so that people would not only get the news, but comprehend the awful significance of the imminence of a horrible and devastating war.

The value of these broadcasts was far-reaching. It was pointed out by the newspapers in England that the people of Europe were not getting the real news unless they were lucky enough to have the equipment to pick up the programs being sent out by American broadcasters. Perhaps back in 1914, if we had had the facilities we have today, it would have been possible to prevent a war that cost millions of lives and untold suffering and privation.

Would that radio could have prevented World War II! This program was destined to be one of the most heard and most important during that war.

So, realizing the tremendous influence of radio, I am more than ever eager to bring you on these noonday talks, the friendship and help that women can always give to one another. Talking over problems, talking up subjects that may provide all of us with a little food for thought, discussing the things we're interested in, whether it's current events or cookery. We'll talk about children, too, and housekeeping, and all the factors that are the backbone of our American homes today. Now and then I'll give you little stories I've picked up from the lowly and the great, bits of color about people and places around New York. And, whenever I can, I'll introduce some of my friends to you. Maybe it'll be the man who sells hot roasted chestnuts over near my office, or perhaps it'll be a famous personality I know you'll be interested in meeting. We'll talk about plays, and motion pictures, and books, too. Yes, we'll get together and discuss our hopes, and our dreams, and our problems.

For instance, here's a problem of mine, and I'd like to know what you think about it. I've been told recently that the majority of women who listen to radio at this time of day want to be entertained. They want gossip about recipes and curtains and fashions, and things like that. And I agree, but I don't think that's ALL they want. I don't think you folks want only the "whipped cream" with your dessert. Maybe you'd like a little plain homemade bread and butter sometimes. In other words, it's fun to talk about gardens and clothes and recipes, but I also believe firmly that you want to hear things now and then that MAKE YOU THINK. Nobody can ever convince me that we women don't have ideas beyond the kitchen. I think we're capable of clear, honest thinking, and that we're decidedly interested in the problems that are facing this chaotic world today. I believe we have views, and good, sane, practical ones, too, on national and international affairs especially as they affect the health, education, and well-being of our youth, our homes, and our communities. And no one can tell me otherwise!

And now, I've got something else I want to tell all of you. It's about the hobby show that's now going on here in New York—

TED COLLINS:
Kathryn, I don't like to interrupt, but do you see that clock?

KATE SMITH:
Oh! Oh! (short) Well, I'm going to that hobby show this afternoon, and I'll tell you all about it on Thursday. I'm on my way, but I'll be with you all day after tomorrow—at noon! Until then, thanks for listenin', and good-bye, folks.

TED COLLINS:
You have been listening to Kate Smith, brought to you each Tuesday, Thursday, and Saturday, at NOON, by the makers of Diamond Crystal Shaker Salt. This is Ted Collins, bidding you good-afternoon.

KATE SMITH DIAMOND CRYSTAL PROGRAM #15 (CBS)
THURSDAY, NOV. 10, 1938

Hello, everybody! Here it is Thursday again, and that means I'm here in my blue and silver dressing room at the Columbia Playhouse, just a stone's throw from Times Square, the crossroads of the world. There seems to be a lot of extra special activity outside my door this morning. They're all here: Jack Miller and the boys in our orchestra, our singers, our dramatic actors, and also a number of friends from out of town who have dropped in to say hello and to watch the rehearsals for the big show tonight. One of our very special guests today is Allene Talmey, Editor of the *Vanity Fair* section of *Vogue* Magazine, and a little bit later on I'm going to ask her to meet you folks, but right now let's see what's in the news...

The death of a dictator and the splendid recovery of five little children after their operation are the highlights in the news of the day.

Kemal Ataturk, the father of the Turkish Republic and its virtual dictator, is dead. He passed away at the age of fifty-eight after he had created a modern Turkey out of a backward island. Ahtaturk was a man of the most unusual charms, handsome and magnetic. Women loved him. During the early days of his power he married a girl eighteen years his junior. She was one of Turkey's first modern women, the first to appear in public in such a thing as riding breeches. She was even too modern for Ahtaturk. He thought she was inclined to be too masterful, so he divorced her by his own decree after two years. Then he lived as a bachelor, but a gay one. His energy was a matter of astonishment. He said he owed his good health to his dancing and poker playing.

The five little Dionnes are all abed today with sore throats, but I'm happy to report that they are all are on the road to recovery from their tonsil and adenoids operations. They aren't quite sure what happened to them but good Doctor Dafoe told them they would feel better from now on. "They're simply excellent," he said this morning.

In Germany, the Nazis are taking vengeance for the killing of an official by a Jewish youth. Mobs roamed the cities and towns last night, wrecking Jewish shops and setting fire to synagogues. It was a night of terror for German Jews.

It's a different story in London. Prime Minister Chamberlain told the people he wants the British Government to be a "go getter" for peace. And he added that conditions in Europe now are settling down to quieter times.

There is good cheer in the United States today with the return of the traditional two-party system, for the Republicans have arisen from almost nothing to a strong minority in politics. Stocks are on the rise and business seems reassured.

In New York, John Dolanchuk, the man without a country, also is without a ship to travel on. The United States Line grew tired of taking him back and forth across the Atlantic free of charge because no country would let him land. So today the liner *President Roosevelt* sailed away, leaving Dolanchuk on the pier. So it's up to the immigration authorities to decide what comes next.

(FIRST COMMERCIAL)

Not so very long ago, a young girl journeyed to New York City to make a career for herself. Her one burning ambition was to write. She succeeded in getting a job as a cub reporter on the *New York World*, and from early morning until late each night she chased all over town getting stories for her paper. When Herbert Swope, the editor, asked her whether she would like to be a dramatic critic, she answered emphatically: "I should say not, anything but that."

Yet today this young lady is an excellent dramatic critic and a chronic "first-nighter." But she's something more than that—in just a few short years she's risen to the section of *Vogue* magazine. Her name is Allene Talmey. She dropped in at the Playhouse this morning to watch our rehearsal, and I think it would be kinda nice to ask her to join us here on the air. Miss Talmey, tell us something about your work as editor of one of America's foremost magazines.

TALMEY:
Thank you, Miss Smith, but as a matter of fact I dropped over here hoping to ask you a few questions. Over at *Vogue*, you know we usually get interviews, not give them. Besides, it's a rather large order to tell you about my work. I follow the world of music, books, the theatre, the art exhibits, get unusual photographs of outstanding personalities…oh, just all sorts of features that we feel will interest our readers.

KATE:
Well, that sounds like fascinating work, Miss Talmey. But now, tell us something about yourself. I understand that along with your editorial duties, you manage to run a household and look after your husband and your little son. I've heard a great deal lately about this question of marriage and a career. How do you feel about it?

TALMEY:
It's difficult, I'll say that, but it's fun. My little boy, Richard, is just four and a half years old, but already he's beginning to take an active interest in my job as well as his father's work.

KATE:
But how do you manage in your busy life to spend much time with Richard, Miss Talmey?

TALMEY:
I guess I'm what you might call organized. Naturally, I feel that a woman's first duty is to her family, but I've tried to arrange my

life so that I'll have time for my husband and my son and my work, too. I spend at least an hour each morning with my little boy, and every day we have a date from five in the afternoon until he goes to bed at seven. We have lots of fun together. I treat him, with reservations, just as I would a grown person.

KATE:
You mean you talk over your work with him?

TALMEY:
Yes, we talk over plays I've seen, and children's books, and I bring home copies of pictures I've taken, and discuss artists and their work with him. Then on Saturdays and Sundays, his dad and I devote our entire weekend to Richard. We take him to the zoo, and the circus, or any of the hundred and one things that attract a small boy. And I don't believe he ever feels that what you call my "career" deprives him of the society of his mother.

KATE:
Then you feel definitely that it's possible for a woman to have a career and raise a family, too.

TALMEY:
I certainly do, Miss Smith, and I even go a step further than that in my conviction. I think that often a mother who has a job is able to contribute a great deal in the way of educating her child, and can enrich his life considerably by the contacts and experiences she has in the business world. I think, too, that a job keeps a woman young and active both in mind and body, and that she can give her youngster closer companionship because of these things.

KATE:
Well, Miss Talmey, I don't know much about bringing up youngsters, but I can certainly agree that you must be a grand pal for your boy, and that a job keeps a woman young, for right this minute you don't look a day over twenty yourself.

TALMEY:
Thank you, Miss Smith, you're very sweet. And now if I'm going to get through my work and get back for those two precious hours with Richard this afternoon, I'll have to be on my way.

KATE:
That's right, but drop in and see us again soon. And don't forget to tell Richard that Aunt Kate sends her love.

(SECOND COMMERCIAL)

The story goes that Diogenes spent his life looking for an honest man, but maybe if he'd searched for an honest woman, his quest would have been more successful. Out in Cedar Rapids, Iowa yesterday, an unidentified woman found a purse containing $9,300 in cash. Without an instant's hesitation she returned the money to its owner, who earlier had reported her loss to the police, and went on her way, That's the kind of little story in the news that it's a pleasure to report, and I only wish I knew the name of the woman who found the purse. But that's the way with people who instinctively do the right thing; they seldom ask for applause.

Tomorrow we pay tribute to our honored dead and to the millions of veterans of World War who were spared to return to their native land following the Armistice of twenty years ago. It has been my privilege to be on the air each Armistice Day or Armistice Eve for the past eight years, and on these occasions I have tried to give a fitting salute to our heroes. This year with the war clouds of Europe so lately threatening the peace of the entire world, I felt I wanted to do something special—something that would not only be a memorial to our soldiers, but would also emphasize just how much America means to each and every one of us. I wanted more than an Armistice Day song, I wanted a new hymn of praise and love and allegiance to America, so several weeks ago, I went to a man I have known and admired for many years, the top ranking composer in the music field today. I explained as well as I could what I was striving for. He said:

"Kate, you want something more than a popular song. I am not sure, but I will try." He worked day after day, night after night until at last his task was completed. The other day he sent me his masterpiece, and along with it this little note: "Dear Kate, here it is. I did the best I could, and it expresses the way I feel."

The song is called "God Bless America." The composer, Mr. Irving Berlin. When I first tried it over, I felt here is a song that will be timeless; it will never die. Others will thrill to its beauty long after we are gone. In my humble estimation, This is the greatest song Irving Berlin has ever composed. It shall be my happy privilege to introduce it to our American heroes of the World War. As I stand before the microphone and sing it with all my heart, I'll be thinking of our veterans and I'll be praying with every breath I draw that we shall never have another war. And I'll also be deeply grateful to Mr. Irving Berlin for his beautiful composition, "God Bless America."

Here Kate relates part of the story behind "God Bless America," which she will introduce tonight. Little did she know how it would influence her career and her life!

The 1938 Nobel Prize for literature, worth forty thousand dollars, has just been awarded in Stockholm to an American author, Pearl S. Buck. Almost all of us know and love Mrs. Buck's greatest book, *The Good Earth*. It won the Pulitzer Prize in 1931 and the movie version of it brought Mrs. Buck's message to millions more. And today Mrs. Buck has been honored with the highest distinction that can be given a writer: the Nobel Prize.

Mrs. Buck, you remember, once was an American missionary in China and most of her books have been written about the Chinese. But the emotions she expressed in her works were common to every nation, and those who read her books find in them the traits of human nature that apply to all of us.

In China, Mrs. Buck grew up, and there she was married. She aided her husband in his missionary work, taught in Chinese universities, and bore her husband's two children. In 1922 she found what she had heretofore lacked—time to write, and with the publication of "The Good Earth" she immediately took her place among America's great authors.

And now, I see that I've about used up the time allotted me for this broadcast, and I must leave you for today, but I'll be back with you all again on Saturday. Until then, thanks for listenin' and goodbye, folks.

After she introduced *God Bless America* on the November 10, 1938, Kate Smith House, composer Irving Berlin attended the rebroadcast for the Pacific Time Zone. Here they pose during the filming of the motion picture "This Is The Army," in which Kate appeared re-creating that introduction.

KATE SMITH DIAMOND CRYSTAL PROGRAM #100, SAT. MAY 27, 1939. (END OF SERIES)

Hello everybody!

History is being made this morning by American businessmen and scientists. For right now the giant flying boat, *Yankee Clipper*, is on her way to complete the first commercial flight to Europe and back. And just about the same time that the great Pan-American airliner lands here with half a ton of mail, her sister ship, the *Atlantic Clipper*, will spread her wings over the ocean on the second regular commercial flight to Europe. There will be six of these round-trip flights across the Atlantic. Then the planes will start carrying passengers.

Do you know what five movie actresses live together in a single house; pool all their earnings; and celebrate the same birthday tomorrow? Yes, you're right: the Dionne Quintuplets. On their fifth birthday the girls possess a fortune of nearly $850,000, and today they are receiving hundreds of birthday cards. The cards have been sorted at the nursery and placed in big envelopes bearing their names. Then, each quint will open her own mail. On their fifth birthday, their personalities have shown definite development. Yvonne is still the leader, but now she's running into competition from Annette and Emilie. Emilie is the comedian, Marie's the most warm-hearted, Annette the most determined, Cecile the most precise, and Yvonne the bossiest. And all of them are beautiful and healthy.

(FIRST COMMERCIAL)

A new travel book which is being written for a New York radio firm brings to light the fact that the state of North Carolina seems to have more than its share of amusing oddities. There's the general store of a man known as the Merchant Prince of Ivanhoe, located in Sampson County. No one, the owner included, knows just what goods his store contains, for the simple reason that it's so piled with merchandise that customers are unable to enter. And there's the lost tribe of Chimney Rock Mountain, where, in order to reach their homes, the people have to climb up a steep trail which has in all 725 steps. There's Enfield, a Halifax County town which has "loafing squares" marked off on the sidewalk for loiterers. And "The Little Beans," a couple only four feet tall who operate a country store at a place called "Little Beans Crossroad." This store has counters, furniture, and furnishings, all built in miniature.

(SECOND COMMERCIAL)

Next Tuesday we commemorate one of the most sacred days in American history. And this year Memorial Day takes on an even greater significance, for the past twelve months have been filled with vague threats that we might be dragged into another terrible catastrophe such as befell our nation in 1861 and again in 1917. The history of Memorial Day is shrouded in sadness, but there's also an undeniable sweetness about its origin. When the war between the states came to an end in 1865, people on both sides wore black for years afterward, so great had been the toll of American manhood. The war was over, yes, but anger, hate, and suspicion were rife throughout the country. Then, in 1867, a short paragraph appeared in a New York newspaper. Briefly it described the action of the women of the little town of Columbus, Mississippi. The item was new, because it revealed that the women of the South were showing themselves impartial in their offerings made to the memory of the dead. They had strewn flowers on the graves of Confederate and Federal soldiers alike. Until that time America's feelings were so sharply split that even such a little news item caused a thrill to pass over the country. It was the first sign that the terrible wounds of war were healing. The following year, in May, 1868, two army generals spoke of the matter. A general of the regular army wrote to a general of the retired Grand Army of the Republic. He suggested that the G.A.R. undertake the decoration of graves of those who had died in the war on either side. General Logan of the Grand Army was much impressed with the idea. He set apart May 30th, 1868, as a day for strewing flowers on the graves of the half million war dead. The very beauty of the thought won national appreciation. Legislatures of a number of states designated May 30th as a legal holiday. Then the idea struck fire in the heart of a young lawyer of Ithaca, New York: Francis Miles Finch. He was inspired to write the poem called "The Blue and the Gray," which, as you know, has become associated with Memorial Day. And year by year the idea spread. In 1875 it was recorded in the annals of the Grand Army of the Republic that the "the annual floral decoration of the graves of our soldiers has become a national custom." Thus one of the most beautiful and significant of our American holidays sprang out of the South, and helped to drive out the bitterness which was the aftermath of the Civil War.

Folks, you know I sit here before this microphone today with mixed emotions. I watch the second hand of the studio clock traveling around in its circle, and the thought comes to my mind that in just a few moments, our commentator programs will come to an end for this season.

I say with mixed emotions because the year has been a very, very busy one for me, and naturally, I'm packing my belongings and moving from my New York City apartment up to my summer home at Lake Placid. I'll be busy with my flower gardens and boats, and all the small tasks which are so different from my hurried life here in the city. There'll be picnic suppers cooked over our big outdoor fireplace, and long lazy days of golf, swimming, and tennis; days when I'll just sit quietly in the sun and rest. Those thoughts make me happy. But when I stop and realize that we'll have no more talks on Tuesday, Thursdays and Saturdays for the next few months, that the mailman won't greet me each morning with a big sack full of mail, then I feel kinda sad. I'll miss these broadcasts. You who write to me have taught me a great deal during the past year. You've taught me how much we all depend upon one another for encouragement and sympathy and friendship; what an important part each one of us plays in the lives of others as we go down the years...

There was a time when just singing satisfied me. Being an entertainer was enough, and I still enjoy singing—make no mistake about that. But last spring I began to feel that the bonds of friendship and understanding between my radio listeners and myself would be closer and more satisfying if we could have a few minutes of talk. Many of the letters that came to me brought up problems that could not be answered with a favorite song. They suggested subjects of vital interest to many people, so I decided to try out a little series of programs speaking from my own experience and convictions, not intending to force my views or my ideas of life on anybody, but talking simply and sincerely as one friend to another.

Out of that small, unobtrusive beginning these programs have grown. To my happiness, they have gained in favor as the weeks went by. Our talks on Americanism, on juvenile delinquency, and safety have commanded the attention of the public in a way which proves beyond a doubt what a vast medium for good lies in radio.

There have been other subjects, too, which have met with your hearty response: bits of philosophy, talks on the vital part religion plays in our daily lives, stories and comments which, according to your letters, have helped and cheered many of you. And for that I'm glad. It's been my privilege also to bring to light through our "Salt of the Earth" feature many fine souls whose activities are a beautiful example, a source of inspiration to all of us.

It was on June 9, 1939 that F.D.R. was supposed to have introduced Kate to the King and Queen by "Your Majesties, this is Kate Smith—this is America." In fact, his words were, "Your Majesties, this is Kate Smith, one of the greatest singers."

Now, before leaving you for the summer, I'd like to repeat what

I've voiced so often in the past. In everything I've said on these programs, I've tried to be honest and sincere; tried to present my ideas, thoughts, and conclusions with humility, hoping always to make them worthy of you. A week from next Thursday, in a formal reception at the White House in Washington I shall have the very great honor of appearing before the President and Mrs. Roosevelt, and their Majesties, the King and Queen of England. That invitation is the highest recognition of my work that anyone could offer, and I am thrilled by it. But whatever applause may come to me, whatever honors are bestowed, I know I can never forget the radio friends who have made possible any success that has been mine so far. I want to thank you, one and all, for the way you've received me into your homes, for your many letters, for your unfailing friendship and support. They mean more to me than you'll ever know. And now, until we meet again, thanks for listenin' and good-bye, folks!

The Kate Smith Hour *was broadcast that hot night, and Kate made radio history by singing her songs from a microphone in D.C. while the orchestra was back in New York. On the rebroadcast for the Pacific Coast, she deviated from keeping both broadcasts identical by telling the audience about her Command Appearance at the White House. (see pages 91-92)*

Kate the Great

The undisputed first lady of radio as of 1939 is 235-lb., 29 year-old contralto Kate Smith. For eight successful radio years Kate Smith has used her booming, unschooled voice, plus occasional bursts of hearty Americanism, to sell millions of dollars worth of cigars, automobiles, coffee and, since 1937, General Foods cake flour, baking powder, and salt. From her paychecks she has tucked away $1,000,000 mostly in Government bonds, but she is still unmarried, lives alone. She has won 15,000,000 weekly listeners, but she can count scarcely a dozen intimate friends.

Last week this publicly expansive first lady was guaranteed her radio job, at a salary of at least $7,000 a week for three more years, in a non-cancellable contract the like of which has been written in radio only once before (for Jack Benny two years ago). Most radio contracts, no matter what their other terms, are cancellable at 13-week junctions. Kate's may be suspended, but only in case of war.

Thirteen years ago Kathryn Elizabeth Smith was an uninhibited 16 year-old lummox of a girl singing and doing the Charleston in Washington, D.C. amateur shows. Broadway showman Eddie Dowling brought her to Manhattan as "Tiny Little" in *Honeymoon Lane.* During more than four years of Broadway (*Hit the Deck, Flying High*), the comics of the show business treated her to so many cruel fat-lady gags that finally, bitter and hurt, she packed and went home.

But a phonograph recording executive named Ted Collins, believing she had better assets than her figure, put her in radio. Simplicity, Collins decided, would put her over. So her introduction became simply: "Hello everybody, this is Kate Smith," her farewell: "Thanks for listenin'."

Soon Kate was giving a fine account of herself in CBS's then-toughest spot, competing for listeners with NBC's Amos and Andy. She dedicated programs to shut-ins, plugged firemen's benefits, camps for the under-privileged, visited cripples, became radio's No. 1 Benefit Girl. To "expand her prestige as an outstanding American Woman" Collins last year arranged a three-a-week noon-day broadcast of homely comment, book & play criticism. Sensitive to the rising tide of Broadway patrioteering, Kate last year got Irving Berlin to write "God Bless America" exclusively for her, sang it week after week until last month, when it was released to other patrioteers.

An informal moment as they confer about today's broadcast, drinking Sanka coffee.

KATE SMITH SPEAKS —
MONDAY, JUNE 24TH, 1940

Because of the program's popularity CBS insisted that it continue through the summer. Ted and Kate said, "only if we can do it from Lake Placid." Cables were strung, a tiny studio was built from a closet in the guest house, and starting today—KATE SMITH SPEAKS *from her Camp Sunshine, on Buck Island in Lake Placid.*

Hello, everybody! I'm speaking to you this morning from Lake Placid, N.Y., where we've set up a complete broadcasting unit. This makes it possible for me to run away for a weekend now and then and still not take any chance of missing my daily talk with you. And you know, I never cease marveling at this wonderful invention that like some magic wishing-ring carries my voice all over the country from anywhere I happen to be. At the moment, incidentally, it almost seems as though I'm in a lovely, faraway world. In New York City, I suppose the traffic is streaming noisily up and down, back and forth, that factories, offices, and other great wheels of industry are grinding busily as usual. Yet here in this quiet spot with no sound but the song of birds, and an occasional voice calling through the silence, one forgets almost everything except the beauty of a blue sky overhead; a cool breeze rustling through the sweet pines; a slender plume of clean, white smoke curling out of a chimney. There's a great wood fire crackling on our hearth this morning to, as they say up in these parts, "sorta take the chill off." To me, it does more than that; it gives me a feeling of home. It's exactly as it should be; a fireplace should always have a fire glowing. And, I'm particularly happy this morning. Ever since I arrived on Saturday, there's been the excitement that always goes with opening a house for the season. Whether it be a big, pretentious estate or a little log cabin in the woods. I walk around discovering little trinkets that I'd almost forgotten. I thrill all over again to the beauty of the view framed by the windows. I go from room to room renewing acquaintance with the books, the pictures, and all the dear familiar objects that make a house into a home. And in my garden, well, on such a morning as this, in such a place, I say: "Oh, it's good to be alive!"

(OPENING COMMERCIAL)

And now, Ted, What's new?

(NEWS)

Well, I see by the papers that young men, and old ones, too, who wish to brush up on the techniques of handling a broom and a mop can now enroll at Teachers College in New York for a course in which a staff of experts, including four college professors, will offer intensive training in sweeping floors, cleaning woodwork, polishing furniture, and other janitors' chores. The course, which requires a $10 tuition fee and a willingness to learn was announced last week. After five days of lectures, demonstrations, round-table conferences, and personal consultations the qualifying students will receive certificates suitable for framing. You know, I can't help chuckling over this piece of news. It's getting so these days that no matter what you want to do, you must have a college course. Here women for centuries and centuries have been quietly going about the business of cleaning, sweeping, scrubbing, washing, and all the other details which attend the running of a household, and men have been accepting these ministrations and giving the so-called weaker sex very little credit for brains, and now the husky male must need have a college course in order to insure proficiency! I suppose next they'll be giving degrees in the art of rocking the cradle with a minimum of effort, and how to streamline the operation of getting little Jimmy started off to school! We certainly do live and learn in this modern age!

(CLOSING COMMERCIAL)

A woman with sightless eyes, and a cook-book: a little cook book containing my own favorite recipes. You wouldn't think there would be much in common between a blind woman and a printed page, would you? But let me tell you a story, a story of how the two came together through the kindness of two big organizations.

Years ago, people everywhere accepted the thought that blindness was an affliction which was an insurmountable obstacle to a useful life, but the sightless have ever been a courageous group. They were unwilling to accept the idea that they should be forever totally dependent upon a busy world. And, encouraged by such dauntless souls as Helen Keller and others among the blind, they began to reach out and find things that they could do with their hands. Some studied music, others typewriting, plastic arts, weaving, knitting, and kindred crafts. Gradually they came to the lovely realization that sightlessness did not mean that they could have no part in active life. Many among the women found that they could manage household tasks and serve their families just as other women did who had the use of their eyes. Many letters have come to me from the blind, letters which told of their ability to cook and their wish that they could read my favorite recipes in our cook book. Last February a listener in North Carolina wrote me about having a blind couple for supper. She spoke of the wife who said she was going to send for one of my cook books and ask someone to read the recipes to her so she could learn to cook good things to eat for herself and her sightless husband. Just think of the ambition of such a woman…think of what it means to learn recipes entirely by heart! Well, that little letter and others like it started a train of thought, and thought started action.

Today, through the generosity of the American Red Cross and the cooperation of my sponsors, my favorite recipes are available in Braille. The first book was transcribed for a blind woman in Pittsburgh, and with the aid of this book in Braille she has already taught five sightless girls to cook and is working with a sixth.

So you see, a blind woman and a printed page can combine into a life of usefulness, and so happiness. I tell you this not in a commercial sense to advertise my cook books, for these books are available only through the American Red Cross in Washington, D.C. and will be shipped postpaid anywhere in the United States for the small amount of 30 cents. I'm glad that a big organization like the Red Cross and a huge food company like my sponsors have given thought to the home-makers and house-keepers with sightless eyes. This is another step forward for the blind.

The words of that immortal English poet of the seventeenth century, John Milton, in his poem "On His Blindness," were very beautiful and comforting but no longer do those who dwell in darkness need to say with him, "They also serve who only stand and wait."

And now, I see it's time for me to be on my way, but I'll be back with you all again tomorrow. So until then, thanks for listenin,' and good-bye, folks!

Ted Collins and Irving Berlin, Nov. 10, 1938.

KATE SMITH SPEAKS —
TUESDAY, DECEMBER 10, 1940

Hello, everybody! This is not a bullfrog you hear, but me, with my old "shadow" laryngitis, the "bugaboo" of all public singers and speakers.

Kathryn's only sister, Helena, 2½ years older, married Lee Steene, an airline pilot who would become a WWII Army Air Corps pilot. They had two daughters. Lee died in 1967. This is a case where Kate did not believe "the show must go on."

I feel somewhat like a truant this morning because yesterday instead of taking my usual place at the microphone, I was down home in Virginia. Often we speak of radio and stage folks being good troopers and sticking to their posts no matter what happens in their private lives, but I'm just old-fashioned and sentimental enough to feel that family ties take precedence over everything else. So, when my only sister told me not long ago that she had set the date for her wedding for Monday, December 9th, I made up my mind that nothing would stop me from being right on hand for that great occasion. The wedding yesterday was a quiet one: just the family and a few friends; a little laughter and a few tears. We threw rice and kissed the bride, and followed the traditions that make weddings something to remember through the years.

And before I forget it, thank you, Mr. C. for doing the program all by yourself—I'll do the same for you sometime.

(OPENING COMMERCIAL)

And now I think I might remind you (as I did remind myself with calendar in hand this morning), that there are only 13 shopping days left before Christmas, and that's counting today. Often, our difficulty with a Christmas list isn't that we don't have time to go shopping, but that when we do go, we wander aimlessly through the stores, looking wildly in every direction for an appropriate gift for Aunt Kit, or Brother George, or little Mary, or great-uncle Ben. We spend hours this way, when a very simple and satisfactory answer to our problem would be a good book. There are any number of fine books on the market. For children there's Rachel Field's little story called *All Through the Night*, which tells of that first Christmas in the manger long ago when the Christ-child was born. For the young naturalist there's a fascinating book called *The Beaver Twins*, and how these velvet brown little animals live, and work, and build in the quiet places in the deep woods. In fact, there are hundreds of good books for youngsters. As for grown folks, almost any man or woman either would like Kenneth Roberts's latest book, *Oliver Wiswell*, a story of the American Revolution by the author of *Northwest Passage*. Or Mary Roberts Reinhart's mystery novel, *The Great Mistake*. For humor combined with wisdom I mention again two books I've spoken of recently: *Mrs. Miniver* and *The McKennys Carry On*, both grand reading. The outstanding poetry volume of the current season is Edna St. Vincent Millay's *Make Bright the Arrows*, for those who like beautiful verse. And I mustn't forget to mention that greatest of all bestsellers, written in prose that is matchless, which carries a message for young and old: *The Holy Bible*. The best way to choose a book is to go to a book shop and take your time. Look them over carefully, and think about them a little bit before deciding which to get for whom, and truly, this is one shopping trip you're bound to enjoy.

(NEWS)

And now that Ted has told what's new, I'm going to speak of something old: the delightful American custom of sending packages, cards, and letters to loved ones at Christmas. Every year about this time, I get a little note from the Postmaster General, asking me to pass along to you a message about those frequently forgotten men, the Postal Clerks, who work early and late during the holiday season. And so, on behalf of the Post Office Department, I want to remind you now to mail early. We all ought to do that, not only to help the mailmen, but to make sure our gifts reach their destination well before the big day.

(CLOSING COMMERCIAL)

And now, I see it's time for me to be on my way, but I'll be back with you all again tomorrow. So until then, thanks for listenin,' and good-bye, folks!

Mr. Collins and Miss Smith are breaking their fast with bowls of Post's Grape Nuts cereal.

KATE SMITH SPEAKS — THURSDAY, MAY 1, 1941

It's the tenth anniversary of Kate's first CBS broadcast, and nary a word is said about it!

Hello, everybody! Well, today is May Day, the beginning of that magic month famous in song, story, and legend, time of flowers and May baskets, of Maypole parties and dancing on the village green. And also, in strange comparison with all the lovely customs of May Day, it's the time these modern days in the large cities when the parks and public squares are the scene of meetings, soap-box orators, and crowds of people haranguing on all sorts of subjects which seem important to various groups and organizations. When I mention these latter-day May Day activities, mind you, I'm not criticizing free speech or those who take part in the demonstrations. But sometimes, when I see the noisy crowds milling about and hear fragments of the speeches made by men and women gathered together to voice complaints and to discuss ways and means of changing conditions in this lovely land of ours, I can't help having a nostalgic feeling for those other May Days, years ago, when the parks and public squares were filled with happy youngsters, dancing around beribboned Maypoles, playing games, and laughing and shouting in the sunshine. Times change and customs change, I suppose. New ways and new people find expression. That's progress. And yet, I'm filled with wonder sometimes to think how much fault is found with a country that to me, compared with other countries and other forms of government, seems nothing short of Paradise. I wonder if all those who seek to change the pattern of our Democracy will ever realize just how lucky they are to be living here in America.

(OPENING COMMERCIAL)

Yesterday, I was the guest of a group of twenty stewardesses at a luncheon they gave at the American Airlines Building out at La Guardia Field. It was one of the most delightful experiences ever, for to have a chance to sit and dine with such a typically American group of young ladies is indeed an inspiration. These girls, presided over by Hazel Brooks, chief instructress, represent all parts of our country, from the smallest cities to the largest. Their outlook is such that you leave with the greatest optimism about the future knowing that within the hearts of these enterprising girls rests the courage and foresight of our greatest pioneers. Their vocation is the most fascinating, and one in which I am perfectly in accord. I hope that the pleasure of such a visit is mine soon again.

And now, Ted, what's new?

(NEWS)

On my desk this morning, I have a letter from the United Hospital Fund of New York. They do not ask for money; they do not ask that we sacrifice or do without. Their request is simply this: If you have any books you do not want, won't you please send them to the Hospital Library Bureau, at 370 Lexington Avenue, New York City, and if it is not convenient to send them, will you send a message to the Bureau, so that they can pick them up? Many of you, I'm sure, have novels of romance, adventure, and mystery; books that are gay, amusing, and entertaining that you've enjoyed reading and that are now standing on a shelf or lying neglected on a table, books you'll never need or want again. It would be a simple thing to pass them along for others to read; others who are shut away from the world sick, discouraged, and alone. Why not, during this time of spring cleaning, get them together and send them today to the Hospital Library Bureau, 370 Lexington Avenue, New York City? They'll be appreciated more than you know.

(CLOSING COMMERCIAL)

The road of the pioneer and the trail blazer has never been easy, and perhaps the most difficult and agonizing of all the efforts of the pioneers of industry, has been the role of the inventor.

George Alexander Hughes was no exception. It was the summer of 1910 in St. Louis, where the electric light and power company executives of the company were holding a convention. Across the aisle from the small booth Mr. Hughes had rented on borrowed money to exhibit his brain-child, was the booth of the biggest electrical company in the world. The man in charge of the huge exhibit told the young inventor he must be crazy—because he was demonstrating what he called "an electric range." "It won't work," they told him. The obscure young man from North Dakota was the object of pity among all the people at the show back in 1910, or perhaps I should say almost all. The convention crowds watched Mr. Hughes cooking on his little electric range. They sampled the delicious foods which he prepared, and now and then some small power company representative would whip out a check book and order one of the strange new contraptions, just so they could try it out!

That was in 1910. Today is my birthday and right here on a table in my living room stands a magnificent birthday cake, presented to me by this same Mr. Hughes, and baked on the one-millionth electric range to be turned out in America! But the story of toil, discouragement, patience and determination that mark the years between that first little electric stove produced in 1910, and the efficient, shining, one-millionth range I've just mentioned, was one of which any man might well be proud.

Mr. Hughes is now the Chairman of the Board of the Edison General Electric Appliance Company of Chicago, better known as the Hotpoint Company, an organization of which he has been President since its founding. The poor inventor with an idea has become one of our outstanding engineers and executives. He has contributed to modern living such appliances as the toaster, the electric heater, the electric iron, the dish washer, and perhaps most important of all, the electric range.

America owes much to its pioneer inventors like George Alexander Hughes, because it is men like these, men from the ranks who have used their brains, their energy, and their vision to contribute better living conditions, greater efficiency, and more comfort to the people of our country, than you'll find anywhere else in the world!

And now, I see it's time for me to be on my way, but I'll be back with you all again tomorrow. So until then, thanks for listenin' and good-bye, folks!

Kate with her cocker spaniel, Freckles.

II
WARTIME

1. TUESDAY, DECEMBER 9, 1941. Americans react to war.

2. TUESDAY, MAY 19, 1942. Wartime in New York City; first broadcast ending with the reminder, "Remember, if you don't write, you're wrong!"

3. TUESDAY, OCTOBER 6, 1942. Kate is in the midst of her first radio war bond marathon.

4. THURSDAY, JANUARY 21, 1943. Kate returns to the air after an absence of nearly two weeks, due to a severe gall bladder attack. Ted Collins gives the closing commentary.

5. TUESDAY SEPTEMBER 21, 1943. Again it's Kate Smith Bond Day at CBS. Story of a soldier wounded on the battlefield.

6. DECEMBER 24, 1943. Christmas Eve—on the *Kate Smith Hour*— for the military. A Christmas message.

*7. WEDNESDAY, JUNE 7, 1944. It's D-Day +1. America's reaction to Invasion Day. Kate reads the lyrics to the Battle Hymn of the Republic.

8. THURSDAY, JULY 13, 1944. "There is a mood to summer days."

9. MONDAY, AUGUST 14, 1944. "To keep the faith." In hindsight we know that the war would end a year from this day.

10. MONDAY, JANUARY 1, 1945. On New Year's Day Kate reviews the events of 1944

11. FRIDAY JANUARY 5, 1945. Kate speaks of the pleasures of a coal stove and tells of a Maine hero and eternal vigilance.

12. TUESDAY, JANUARY 30, 1945. It's FDR's 63rd birthday. She speaks about returning servicemen after the war.

13. FRIDAY, APRIL 13, 1945. The President is dead.

14. THURSDAY, APRIL 26, 1945. About Kalamazoo and a clown named Little Danny Sullivan.

15. MONDAY, APRIL 30, 1945. False reports of victory in Europe. Italy's dictator Benito Mussolini is dead.

16. TUESDAY, AUGUST 14, 1945. Victory over Japan? Prisoners of war.

17. WEDNESDAY, AUGUST 15, 1945. Victory over Japan indeed! The lessons of war.

(*) On CD

KATE SMITH SPEAKS —
TUESDAY, DECEMBER 9, 1941

Americans react to the shock of the Pearl Harbor attack and declaration of war yesterday.

Hello, everybody! Yesterday and Sunday were days that no American now living can ever forget. The stirring words of the President of the United States are etched in our memory forever. We, as a nation, grieve for those who already have given their lives in defense of our country. We go forward now with one common purpose. The days to come are going to require all the effort of heart and hand that we are capable of giving. These are facts which we accept without flinching. The road may not be an easy one to travel. It may take many long months to accomplish. It will mean anxious hearts, but it will also reveal courageous hearts. Our strength will be tried, but it will not be found wanting. Our record in the past has been a flaming torch that has lighted the path of freedom. That freedom is being threatened now, but it cannot be destroyed. Millions of men and women have in the past sacrificed everything they held dear, everything save honor, to preserve liberty. Millions of us now stand ready to offer the same sacrifices so that liberty many not vanish from this earth. These are not empty words, not merely oratorical utterances based on what we would like to believe: they are the pulsing voice of America sweeping across this broad land and all of its outposts. Ask the man who drives the truck or the taxi in your town; talk to the men and women in offices and factories; go to the mothers of this nation; speak with the very young and the very old (two groups who, up to now, haven't said very much about America's destiny in this tragic pattern that has unfolded and spreads today over the world). You'll find the reassuring answer on the lips of men and women in all walks of life, from the home-maker to the laborer and mechanic, from the bookkeeper to the doctor, the lawyer, and the minister in the pulpit.

I talked with a dozen women yesterday afternoon. I talked with men, too: elevator operators, theatrical booking agents, musicians, the grocer behind the counter, the little old lady at the news-stand. And in effect, every one of them said the same thing: "We have a job to do. We may not like it; as a nation, we hate war. But we have never been a people to shirk an unpleasant job. Let's get on with it."

That's the consensus of opinion in the circle I've contacted. You'll find it identical in yours. And though, as intelligent people, we do not discount the difficulties of our task, there is no doubt in our minds as to the outcome. I know you are all waiting for out latest bulletins. I'll be back with you later, but now, here is Ted Collins to tell us what's new.

(NEWS)

You have just heard the news, news that must only intensify our strength of purpose and our determination. The one bright spot on our horizon today is the mass awakening of America's millions to a power and unity no force on earth can destroy.

As for me, I pledge myself anew to perform to the best of my ability, and to the limit of my capacity, everything I am called upon to do for my country. Meantime, the work at hand is to speak to you each day on these programs, just as I always have. I shall continue to bring you stories of places and people. We will talk from time to time of books and plays, of the Christmas season so close at hand, of the giving of gifts and the reunion of families, of our hopes and our dreams, our homes and our shopping. We will not become so preoccupied with war and the news of war that we lose our perspective or forget our optimism. We have a need to seek forgetfulness now and then from the cares of these days. We must not lose our ability to laugh and be gay, to sing and to play. These are also treasures we need to guard and guard well. Light hearts and stout hearts we'll preserve—they also are weapons which will confound our enemies.

Ted Collins will continue to give you, each day, clearly and concisely as usual, the very latest news. You can depend upon him for that, and you can depend upon me to continue to give you the best I have always: my hand as a hand in yours, in friendship and communion, reaching out to you, touching you gently, and saying "We are not alone. We have God, and right, and we have one another. Let us go forward with nobility, dignity and serenity. This, too, will pass."

And now, I see it's time for me to be on my way, but I'll be back with you all again tomorrow So, until then, thanks for listenin' and good-bye, folks!

Kate and her maternal grandparents, the Hanbys, in 1940.

KATE SMITH SPEAKS —
TUESDAY, MAY 19, 1942

The wartime scenario in Manhattan.

Hello, everybody! Yesterday and last evening, I took a good look at this big town of New York, and I have to report that news on this home front is that war is certainly leaving its mark everywhere, and people seem to be accepting curtailments cheerfully, which is a good sign. Our city streets aren't the traffic-packed thoroughfares they used to be. It's almost a temptation to do some jaywalking with the wide open spaces in the majority, but I still obey the lights. And speaking of lights, New York hasn't any gay-white-way anymore; it's still gay, but not white. Beginning with last evening, dim-out regulations were in full force, with advertising lights, neon signs, floodlights, and other outdoor lighting out down considerably. Street, bridge, and park lights aren't the blazing strings of jewels they used to be, either. But we take it in our stride because it's not only a necessary precaution against the enemy, but it will certainly result in a material saving of current. In most of our stores yesterday, signs were displayed stating that goods were being sold according to the regulations called "ceiling prices," and it seemed to me there were many good bargains, especially in house wares and clothing. I notice, too, that city parks do not have their quota of May parties this spring, although youngsters still play on the grass, the boys still play ball after school, and those who can spare the time sit on the benches and on the green enjoying the good outdoors and the lengthening days. War can't stop spring, even if this year we are much too busy to give way to spring fever! And while we work and sacrifice now, we can dream happily of other springs to come in this loveliest land on earth.

(OPENING COMMERCIAL)

Last Sunday afternoon, as many of you probably heard, we signed off our "Spirit of '42" broadcast from the United States Marine Base at Quantico, Virginia, with these words: "If you don't write, you're wrong." Since then we have received many letters asking us just what was the meaning of "If you don't write, you're wrong" so I'll try to explain it to you briefly.

Kate explains her wartime reminder given at the end of each broadcast, "if you don't write, you're wrong."

This explanation is only intended now for every American who doesn't wear a uniform, and it's about every American who does. By that I mean Marine, Soldier, Sailor, Aviator, Coast Guard, Merchant Marine, and all of the men fighting for us away from home. I tell you now, it is of great importance that you write to the boys. Write every single day to your loved ones or your friends in service. Tell them anything pleasant that is happening at home. It may seem trivial to you, but I talked about this matter over with fifty different young men training in the Marine Corps on Sunday afternoon and they all told me when they get a letter from home, sometimes they read it as many as a dozen times. So please remember everybody, the men who are ready to die for us live for our letters, and if you would like to adopt my words as a slogan to pass on to all of your friends, this is it: Remember, if you don't write, you're wrong.

(NEWS)

And now briefly, here are a few items on the lighter side of war news:

Down at an Alabama flying field, a young English flying cadet was guided by an American buddy to a lunchroom. The British flier stared at the toothpick which held his hamburger together, then blurted: "The blooming thing has a splinter in it!"

And here's another story from the South, which shows that no matter how thoroughly our lives are regimented these days, personality still crops up. When one soldier at an Army camp in the South writes a letter home, he not only prints the word "free" where the stamp would ordinarily go, but he adds with a flourish directly underneath, "Thank You."

We also learn that the Dutch girls are refusing to get chummy with the Nazi soldiers. One soldier had quite a case on a Holland lassie, but she was unsympathetic. "Why can't we be friends?" he entreated. "What is it that's keeping us apart?" She told him in just one word: "Rotterdam."

And now since I mentioned the Nazi, here's a little item about the Japs. According to Lou Costello, who used to say "I'm a bad boy" on our Kate Smith Shows, we would be willing to divide the Pacific Ocean with the Japs. "We'll each take half," says he. "We'll take the top half and give them the bottom!"

TED COLLINS:
Which sounds like an excellent idea!

(CLOSING COMMERCIAL)

A couple of weeks ago in Pittsburgh, an eight-year-old boy was sure his young life was permanently shrouded in the blackest of black clouds. He had a dog and the dog's name was "Schnappsy," and the boy and his dog were a pair that needed no introduction to happiness. His father had found the dog last winter and took him in out of the cold to feed him. It was pals at first sight with the youngster and the dog; they've been inseparable. But the story took a bad turn two weeks ago. The animal's rightful owner appeared and heart-breaking things happened afterward. Would the dog recognize his real master? Would it go to the feet of the woman who prized it, or to the boy who had befriended it? Well, justice was served, for the woman who claimed ownership was able to prove it to the satisfaction to the judge, and so the boy said good-bye to Schnappsy with tears and a heavy heart.

More than one heart was moved by that decision that parted boy and dog, and I mean now the heart that beats behind the judicial robes of Judge Andrew T. Park. He looked from his bench and said, "You find yourself another dog, young man, and you can count on me to pay for it."

Well, that kindly gesture stirred other hearts. The West Penn Kennel Club has just promised to give the boy one of the nicest dogs I know of: a cocker spaniel puppy. And with the money Judge Park had planned to spend to buy a dog, he's going to purchase a fifty-dollar War Bond.

What is that old saying about every dark cloud having a silver lining? Well, silver or gold, there's one little boy who doesn't want the lining. He doesn't want silver or gold; he's on top of the world right now with a new dog and a war bond. Who could ask for more than that? Hooray for Judge Andrew T. Park.

And now I see it's time for me to be on my way, but I'll be back with you all again tomorrow. So until then, I'll just say thanks for listenin,' and if you don't write, you're wrong. Good-bye, folks!

Kate often typed letters to her radio "friends" (she disliked the word "fan") on her Remington.

KATE SMITH SPEAKS — TUESDAY, OCTOBER 6, 1942

It's Kate's first radio War Bond marathon. She would be credited with selling some $600 million in bonds during the second World War! So successful was she that Columbia University made a study called "Mass Persuasion: The Psychology of a War Bond Drive" (1946).

Hello, everybody! If you should hear during the next fifteen minutes the sound of telephone bells, voices talking away from this mike, or telegraph boys barging in here to the studio, don't mind them, for those noises today are warming my heart! You see, since 6:15 this morning, I've been on the air every few minutes on the New York station urging every person who hears my voice to buy bonds. Ted and I are running an endurance race for Uncle Sam today. We're talking on radio, taking orders by telegraph. Crowds are pouring in to hand over their money and get those blessed bonds, those pieces of paper that are the finest insurance policy for freedom anybody ever had a chance to invest in. So, as I say, If we're a little bit noisy today or a little bit confused, just charge it up to a whole lot of very welcome activity here at the Columbia studios. It's a red letter day, all right, and before we go off the air sometime tomorrow morning, we hope to have sold many war bonds! How are we doin' at the moment, Ted?

TED:
Kate, the orders are coming in so fast that I can't give you the exact figures.

(OPENING COMMERCIAL)

And now, Ted, what's new?

(NEWS)

(CLOSING COMMERCIAL)

"Backward, turn backward, O Time, in thy flight!" How often during these past dreadful months since Pearl Harbor have we whispered that line, turning our thoughts to the peaceful days before the shadow of war spread its dark shape over this land we love. The shadow that has touched almost every little home over the length and breadth of America, that has taken a son or a brother, a husband or a sweetheart, and sent him thousands of miles away to some distant spot where the bombs are dropping, where the tanks are rolling, where the noise and the smoke and the fire of battle are an inferno such as we at home can scarcely imagine. Yes, the youth of America are in there now, in the thick of a fight to conquer mighty, ruthless aggressors whose sole aim is to enslave the world. And you and I, we're here at home thinking of them, writing to them, praying for them, missing them! Missing them, and missing too that sweet peace and serenity that we once knew and accepted lightly as our heritage, as Americans free to pursue our lives in happiness and security.

Remember those carefree, precious times? Remember those days when your son, or your brother, or the lad next door came home every night when the day's work was done? Came home and read the paper, and listened to the radio, and lingered at the supper table, and then, maybe, went to a movie or out in the family jalopy for a ride in the cool of the evening? Remember how you used to step out on the porch a moment before you locked up for the night...the brightness of the stars up there in the peaceful sky above America? Now and then a voice drifted to you on the breeze, a friendly voice saying goodnight to a friend. High overhead the small, winking lights of a plane traced a moving pattern against the heavens. There goes the Transcontinental, you thought to yourself, and in your mind's eye, you envisioned the passengers way up there in the mysterious dark, winging comfortably to their appointed destinations. There was no terror then for you and yours: no terror when the town clock struck the hour, no sudden shock when the telephone rang or the mailman came, for this was America! Yes, this was America, and the dreadful shadow of a swastika and the demented voice of a Nazi leader had not yet touched this stronghold of liberty, had not yet sent the wily Nipponese sneaking over the blue Pacific to tear into shreds the peace of a quiet Sunday morning in December.

But that was yesterday. That was almost a year ago. That was before the war! That was before our lads in navy blue knew the grimness of the order they hear often now: "Man your battle stations!" That was before thousands of our khaki clad soldiers, our devil-dog Marines, our fliers and our sailors, said good-bye. They're in the jungles of Australia now, in the fog and smoke at the Aleutians. They're on the Burma Road and over the English Channel and in the Solomons, and standing watch in the frozen reaches of Iceland, of Alaska. Wherever the action is hottest, wherever the battle rages, you'll find our boys there, their courage and their skill tracing a new glorious pattern in the annals of America—little boys suddenly grown up, a fierce light in their bright eyes, a drumbeat in their valiant hearts, knowing, as they fight, as they give their precious life-blood in their country's cause, that that country is worth the sacrifice. For they're not fighting for a tyrant leader, they're not fighting for conquest, for reward, for medals, or for fame. They're not fighting because the power of an Axis pushes them into the fray. They're fighting, and proud to fight, for you. For the free soil of America. For the right of all humanity to live in peace, and comfort, and security. Fighting so sons and daughters may kneel beside their little beds at night and lift their small, innocent voices without fear as they say: "Now I lay me down to sleep!"

They're fighting and dying, many of them giving their lives for freedom's sake. Do you wonder that I say to you now, and keep on saying, BUY BONDS! Is it too much to ask you, even if you have bought, even if you plan to buy more later, to buy at least one: now, today? Our boys are willing, if need be, to DIE. Can you be less willing, in their name, to BUY? I ask you to think this over and then, if you're in New York City, to walk over to your telephone and call Wickersham 2-1383. I'll be right here at the other end of the wire: ready, eager, grateful for your bond order. I'll answer your call gladly, if you answer America's call NOW. Or if you're outside of New York, send me your pledge by Postal Telegraph. They'll transmit your message free. But whatever you do, whether you telephone or wire, buy a bond from me today. Money talks. But today it does more than talk. It fights. Make your dollars fight for America. And make them speak up even above the noise of battle, telling our boys at the front that we'll never let them down! Will you do that? Thank you!

Thanks for listenin.' And remember: if you don't write, you're wrong. Good bye, folks!

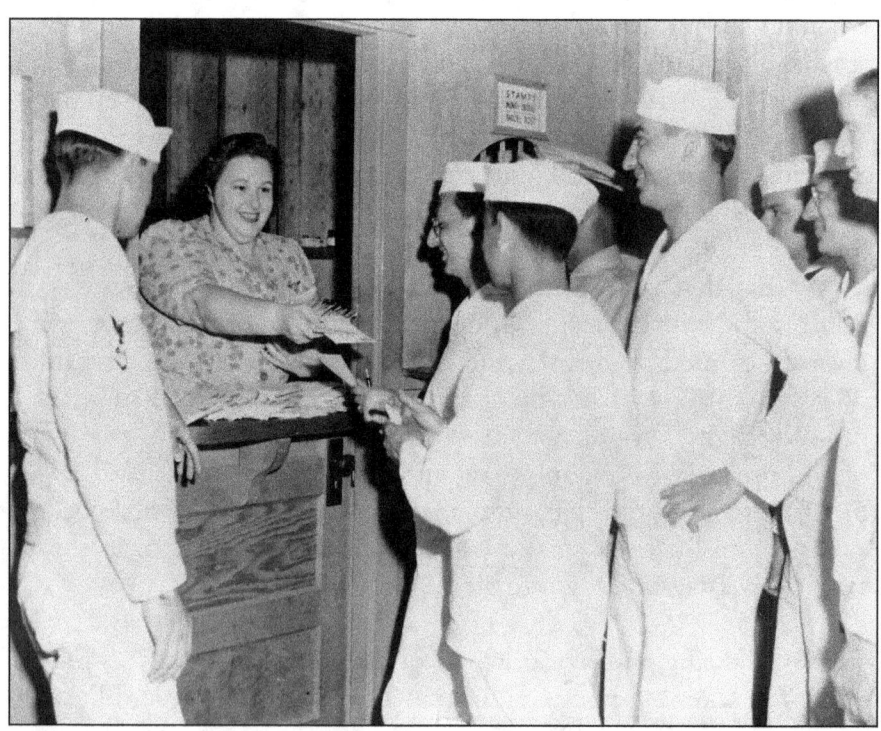

Kate presides at mail call for a group of sailors.

KATE SMITH SPEAKS —
THURSDAY, JANUARY 21, 1943

Kate has been off the air for two weeks, as she suffered a very severe gall bladder attack. Surgery was just barely avoided, and she has controlled the problem all these years by avoiding certain fatty foods, and especially bananas.

It's high noon in New York and time for Kate Smith, who comes to you every day except Saturday and Sunday, with a quarter-hour of news, comments, and stories. Yes, it's high noon, and this is Ted Collins on the job as usual, in this business of radio. When I say "on the job," I really mean it. Bright and early this morning I had a telephone call before 7 a.m. from Charlie Tobias, songwriter, who had a brainstorm. He was sure he had a "hit," and nothing would do but I must hear it right away! It's been my proud boast over the years that I've happened to pick out as naturals quite a few numbers that later swept the nation as hits. Ordinarily I listen while burning the midnight oil, but this morning, after considerable urging, I hurried down-town and heard this new tune just as the early morning sun was climbing up over Manhattan. And believe me when I tell you it's a song worth getting up early to hear! I was sold on the title to begin with. It's called "You're Irish and You're Beautiful!" The music has a swingy lilt, the lyrics are wonderful, and I can scarcely wait to hear Kate Smith sing that song as only as she can sing it. It's surely something to look forward to! And one of these days, maybe a month from now, I'm going to have a chance to say, "I told you so!" Because, take it from me, "You're Irish and You're Beautiful" is going to be a Number One hit! And that starts today off right for me!

(OPENING COMMERCIAL)

And now, ladies and gentlemen, I have with me here what I'd call the world's finest guest star. She needs no introduction! Here she is...Kate Smith!

KATE SMITH:

Hello everybody! No words can ever express how glad I am to be with you all! Time is not truly measured in days or weeks, but by the thoughts that travel through the mind, and it seems years since that Friday of January 8th, when pain first took hold of me and left me puzzled and bewildered and sort of ashamed that I could not hope to carry on as always. But I shan't talk too much now about what's past and done with. Rather I like to speak of the combination of groups of people who have miraculously helped me to make a quick recovery from a serious illness. First and most important, I want to thank each and every one of you who sent me cards, letters, and messages. They are a very real help in bringing back health, because behind them lie the thousands of shining thoughts that reach out and lift up and supply needed strength. Second, I'd like to express my thanks to the very attentive and able physicians who looked after me through this trying period. And lastly, I'd like to reiterate my unshakable and firm belief in the power of prayer. Messages came to me from ministers, rabbis, and priests, telling me they were offering up special prayers for me, and from all over this land came other messages, from plain, every-day folks without titles. They also were praying for me. It is my belief that all these prayers and all these good thoughts directed toward me have done more than medicine! Now, thank God, and I say it reverently, I am myself again. And if my voice is a little bit shaky, well, it's because it's my first day up and I'm excited and tremendously happy to be back! And now, Ted, tell us, what's new?

(NEWS)

(CLOSING COMMERCIAL)

A little while ago I heard someone on the radio yelling "Are you listening to me Hitler—we'll finish you—Hirohito, you rat, and you know, I thought, how foolish. Calling our enemy nasty names isn't going to win this war! We ought to know that from the old, childish chant we used to know back in our childhood days. Do you remember how our deadly small-fry enemies would stand at a safe distance, brandishing their inconsiderable fists, and calling us all manner of impolite names? And how we would sing back smugly, "Sticks and stones will break my bones but names will never hurt me!" Remember? Well, many people in America don't or else they never really believed it anyhow. Because, today, there's much too much name calling going on, too much harmless imprecation being rained down on the enemy. We all should know by now that an enemy that oppresses and tortures helpless civilians is not sensitive, that an enemy who attacks a friendly nation in peace-time as Japan did, is not thin-skinned. Men who are deaf to the cries of women and children directly under their swords are not attentive to imprecations from all the way across the sea. It isn't going to do at all, calling them names. It won't do, just calling the Nazis "rats," or if you're in a particularly tough mood, "dirty rats." It won't do to call the Japanese "slant-eyed devils." They're too busy to listen, and besides, they don't understand English. And it isn't bolstering your own morals, because name-calling is a sign of weakness. So save your breath. Hurling imprecations from now until doomsday will only serve to hasten doomsday...for us! Let's understand completely the nature of our enemy. Let's appreciate once and for all the fact that nothing will penetrate that callous skin of his like high-velocity steel jacketed bullets! That only high explosives will shake him from his power. "Sticks and stones will break their bones." Yes, sticks of bombs from swarms of American planes, stones of Nazi strongholds raining down upon Nazi heads! Those are the things to pour upon the enemy: sticks, stones! Never mind the nasty words and the fist shaking from a safe distance. "Nyah, Nyah, you can't catch me!" is what the little fox said, and that's defensive talk. Let's have the wisdom of the fox , but the power and dignity of the lion, the bear, the eagle, which are the symbols of power and the glory of the great United Nations! Forget that "slant-eyes" talk. Slanted eyes are just as dangerous at a periscope or at a gun-sight as are straight, occidental eyes. Forget calling the Nazis rats. The rat, lest we forget, is an animal that has survived throughout the ages, from prehistoric times. It is a creature made for survival, whatever its many faults may be. A rat isn't nice, but he's dangerous and he has survived all earthly perils. Hate him, revile him, but respect his power of evil. Remember that sticks and stones will break his bones, that names will never hurt him. Save your breath; save it to ask yourself "What did I do today to hurt the Axis?" Save it for saying "I'll have one war bond, please." Save it for all the better purposes you'll need it for before this war is over.

And now, I see my time is up. This is Ted Collins, saying "Remember, if you don't write, you're wrong, and inviting you to join us again tomorrow, WHEN KATE SMITH SPEAKS!"

Kate with a wartime blood donor poster.

KATE SMITH SPEAKS —
TUESDAY, SEPTEMBER 21, 1943

Kate gave War Bond appeals every fifteen minutes for eighteen hours that day. Kate is credited with having sold some $600 million of war bonds during the second World War. This is one of the principal reasons President Reagan presented her with the Medal of Freedom in 1982— the highest honor that can be given to an American civilian.

Hello, everybody! This is Kate Smith again. I say again, because if you've been tuned in on Columbia before today, you'll know I've been on the air at intervals since eight o'clock this morning, sixteen times on various programs at work on an assignment more important than any other job in the world! Yes, it's Columbia Broadcasting's Kate Smith Bond Day today and until tomorrow morning if necessary. As long as my voice holds out, I'm going to be telling America about bonds, and asking America to help, but more about that later! Ted here, who has been right alongside me since long before breakfast, seems to have something on his mind (laughing).

(OPENING COMMERCIAL)

And now, Ted, what's new?

(NEWS)

(CLOSING COMMERCIAL)

All over America, autumn is dancing over the hills and plains, tapping out the rhythm of the changing seasons. All over America, the same dear, familiar beauty is spread as we go about out work and our play. It's football time, and school time, and harvest time. Time of state fairs and the opening of new plays. Time of shopping for winter clothes, time of looking forward to Thanksgiving and Christmas. We are at war, we're working harder, we're missing many dear ones, but otherwise our busy beautiful world is the same. No bombs pierce the peaceful silence of our night, no smoke hides the glory of our sunsets. No alien hands plunder our possessions or send us off to prison camps in life that is worse than death.

But somewhere, in the mud and grime and noise of the battle-front, a young man in khaki lies sprawled on unfamiliar earth. He lies very still and in his eyes there is untold agony. The guns of the enemy have gotten him, and as his comrades plunge forward into the black hell of war, he waits for the stretcher-bearers. He lies very still now. Six feet of strong, husky American manhood; blonde hair tangled with dust and blackened with smoke, brave body stained with blood. He's twenty-one years old, and for fourteen months that seem like centuries, he's been in the thick of battle a long way from home. He was just an average American kid; came from a little town like any other American town: a white church on the hill, a fishing stream winding through the valley, a town hall, and a high-school, and a job in the drug-store on Main Street. He used to play football and basketball and take girls to the dances on Saturday night. He belonged to the village library, and sang in the church choir, and went to the movies over at the Palace. He liked life in his town, liked having breakfast in the kitchen, with Mom frying his eggs and pouring his morning coffee. He liked seeing there, her cheeks rosy, her stout form enveloped in a gingham apron. He liked Sis and the steadfast look in her eyes when she said "I Pledge Allegiance to the Flag of the United States." He liked to hear Dad talk politics and the way he pounded his work-worn fists on the table and said: "No matter how you look at it, there is no substitute for Democracy." He liked racing around in his old Ford, crowding it up with his gang and slipping nickels in jukeboxes and dancing to songs like the "Hut Hut Song" and "Rose O'Day." "I don't want to set the world on fire…" No, he didn't want to set the world on fire. He wanted to live and work and love and get married. He wanted always to be able to watch the sun go down behind those hills of home and walk in the familiar ways all Americans love. He wanted Thanksgiving and Christmas, and trees aglitter with lights, and ice-skating on the pond, and to join his lusty voice with those of his friends. "Holy Night, Silent Night," and sometimes, when the mood was right, harmonizing that perennial favorite, favorite of an earlier time, "Sweet Adeline." That's all he wanted, this boy who now lies very still upon the field of battle. But wait! There was just one more thing, a thing he didn't think about often, but it was there, all right, wrapped close and warm in his heart. That thing called "love of country." He wanted freedom, and liberty, and the kind of a land America had been since its hardy beginnings. That's why he cheerfully turned his back upon all the things he loved: because he was willing and eager to fight, and die, for their preservation.

He's lying wounded on a battlefield now. He doesn't want to be there. He wants to be home, safe in his comfortable clean white bed. He doesn't want to die—nobody wants to die. He didn't like to fight, and shoot, and kill. No decent human being enjoys those things. But he went right ahead. He went ahead for you, and for me, and for millions of Americans who at this very moment are living safe, happy, comfortable lives, making more money than they've ever made before, perhaps. Eating plenty, living the good easy American life every one of us prefers.

Why should he be there, on that blood-stained battle-field? Why should he, and thousands upon thousands of our youth, be carrying the burden? Why, in God's name, should he lay down his precious life on the altar of freedom, while we go our accustomed ways in comfort and safety? Is there any way we can repay him? Is there any way we can even up the score and repay him for even a tiny portion of his sacrifice? If there any way we can get this ghastly war over more quickly for him and his comrades-in-arms? You all know the answer! BACK THE ATTACK! Buy bonds and more bonds; not only as a good investment, not only as a gesture of patriotism, BUT BECAUSE YOU'RE EVERLASTINGLY

GRATEFUL! BACK THE ATTACK with every dollar, every penny you can spare! And be thankful that you're lending your money instead of laying down your life in the cause of victory, and peace!

And now, I see it's time for me to be on my way. But you'll be hearing from me again at intervals for the next fourteen hours, asking you to buy bonds and more bonds, to help us win this war and bring the boys back home. Thanks for listenin,' and remember: if you don't write, you're wrong. Good-bye, folks!

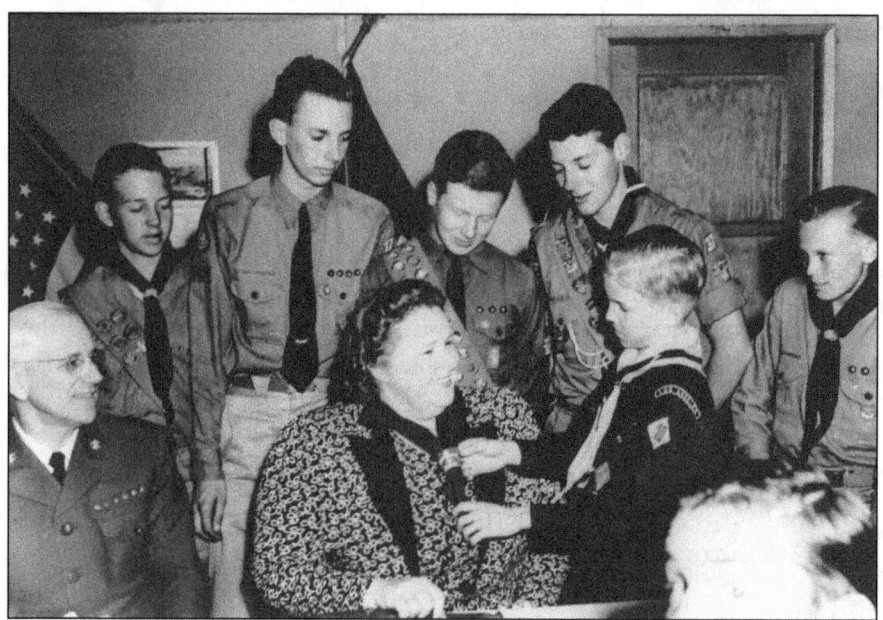

Profits from the performance of *God Bless America* accrued to the Boy and Girl Scouts of America.

KATE SMITH SPEAKS — FRIDAY, DECEMBER 24, 1943

It's our third wartime Christmas.

Hello, everybody! Today, as we rehearse for our "Kate Smith Hour" tonight, there is excitement and the breathless beauty of the holiday season. We have our Christmas greens, and mysterious packages arriving, and greetings are exchanged with friends old and new. We'd like to visit all day but we know we can't, for we have work to do. We smile as we recall the lovely Christmas rhyme, "'Twas the night before Christmas, and all through the house, not a creature was stirring, not even a mouse!" At our Columbia Playhouse tonight, it won't be quiet, and we'll be stirring, all right. There'll be music and laughter and maybe the gift of a tear or two as we offer you, according to custom, the beautiful and sacred story of "The Small One." I'll sing the Christmas songs we love, too: "White Christmas," "Home," "Silent Night," and "Ave Maria." We're going to have a grand Christmas party, and we want each and every one of you to join with us. Let us all, tonight, on this blessed Eve, be together in spirit when the curtain goes up on our "Kate Smith Hour!"

(OPENING COMMERCIAL)

Whatever we're doing today, wherever we are, our thoughts are winging through space to our armed forces in faraway corners of the world, and so it's good to speak of the announcement of the War Department that the makings of a real American Christmas are being flown to servicemen who are stationed in remote areas which only planes can reach. That certainly is good news, and here's more of the same variety: hundreds of evergreens, tons of cigarettes, candy, cake, radios, and recording machines are being distributed to troops from windswept Point Barrow in Alaska to the steaming jungles of New Guinea. Decorated Christmas trees have even been flown the entire 1600 miles of the desolate, treeless, Aleutian chain, where the only native living things are the frozen tundra grass and the scavenger raven. To the tiny weather station in the Bering Sea will go the first mail in four months, dropped from planes into the snow that blankets the area. To the men in the Aleutians will go the second taste of fowl since their arrival: turkey, olives, shrimp, and rolls will be flown to them by planes, and in each far-flung outpost, there will be special services conducted by air-borne chaplains. And it's a comforting thing to know that these things are being done, to let our men in service know we are thinking of them, that we remember.

And now, Ted, what's new?

(NEWS)

(CLOSING COMMERCIAL)

Tonight, just a half hour before the blessed Christmas Eve surrenders to Christmas Day itself, the celestial music of the chimes will ring out from St. Patrick's Cathedral here in New York City. There are 19 bells in all in that north tower two hundred feet above the pavement, and they are famed far and wide as having the purest tones of all the chiming bells in America. Blessed tones, they say, and they are right. These bells were blessed in 1897 by Archbishop Corrigan when they were brought to these shores from Savoy, France, where they had been cast. Yes, promptly at 11:30 the bells of St. Patrick's will carry the message of Christmas halfway across the city, full and clear. Once in the year there is the sudden hush. The gay crowds hurrying down Fifth Avenue pause for a moment. The city somehow seems to hold its breath. And into the lull, above the noise of traffic, the clamor of many voices, clear-throated bells ring out the glad tidings. Thousands of people, people of all creeds, stop and listen to the beautiful strains of "Adeste Fideles," and while they listen, strangers look at one another with a sort of shy kindness, as if they were recognizing their brothers. Then they go smiling on their way, the echo of Yuletide still warm in their hearts, the healing quality of the bells companioning them, renewing hope, repeating a promise, speaking to the lonely, reminding the careless. For at Christmas there is a communion of spirit which draws all of us closer together. I stand here now before this small microphone which is the ear of my invisible audience. I, too, am unseen to you, but I do not feel alone, for I am sure in spirit we are near to one another as I am sure he who came amongst us almost 2,000 years ago is near to us. Tomorrow we celebrate his birth. He came amongst us with a message. There were no newspapers then, or telephones, or radios, yet his simple speech carried to the ends of the earth, sounding high above the trumpets of war, the swing of the lash, and the cries of the oppressed. His teachings have lived, When the Prince of Peace, the Christ-child born in Bethlehem, walked into the market place, it was a time of great stress. Then, as now, the world was torn by wars, by lust for power, by persecution. Yet when he spoke men everywhere listened and rejoiced, for wisdom came from his lips and his brow shone with a solitary radiance in that dark age.

Now, on this Christmas Eve, I have an unutterable longing in my heart to reach out to all of you, to offer a wish, to voice a prayer that will bring peace to your spirit when war lies like a dark shadow across this land of ours, when those we love, like the crusaders of old, have gone forth into danger and death to battle for us. And I do not ask you to forget, because to forget those we love is to forswear the meaning of this holy season. To us who are grown up, this Christmas must mean patience and faith and thoughtful prayer. It must mean bearing our cross cheerfully, keeping the spirit of Christmas for our very young. I hope all of you will have as happy a Christmas as you can; that something will happen in each of your lives to make your day satisfying. And I hope, too, tomorrow (in war as in peace) that Christmas for all little ones will be unclouded; that bells will jingle merrily along the highways of their youthful hearts and that before another Christmas star glitters high in the heavens on Next Christmas

Eve, Americans, young and old will have, for always, the most blessed gift of all good gifts...the gift of victory and lasting peace!

Thanks for listenin.' Merry Christmas, and remember: if you don't write, you're wrong. Good-bye, folks!

Ted Collins and Kate are in what Bob "Believe it or Not" Ripley called the world's smallest broadcast studio, in the guest cottage at Camp Sunshine at Lake Placid.

KATE SMITH SPEAKS —
WEDNESDAY, JUNE 7TH, 1944

It's the second day of the greatest invasion of the War: D-Day+1.

Hello, everybody! Well, Invasion Day has come and gone. The waiting and the tension are over. Now we know that our gallant Armies are fighting on the mainland of Europe, fighting to restore to that enslaved continent its most precious possession: freedom.

As you know, not many celebrations greeted the good news. In fact, most Americans preferred to be by themselves or with their families, and listen to the radio bulletins. But churches all over the country were crowded, with streams of worshipers passing in and out to ask divine protection for their loved ones.

The people of the United States preferred to take D-Day seriously and prayerfully.

There was no confetti, no wild demonstrations. Instead, thousands of Americans responded to the good news in a much finer and better way. Throughout the country, they trooped to blood donor Stations and War Bond booths.

War Bond sales increased. Payroll offices of factories were swamped with bond buyers. Some cities started their fifth war loan drive early, and have already sold their quotas. Yes, Americans are rallying behind our gallant armies of liberation storming fortress Europe, but don't forget for a moment that the war is far from won.

So here on the home front this noon, let's renew our determination to do everything we can to speed the day of victory for our fighting men. Let's volunteer at our blood donor stations again and again. Let's buy more War Bonds and keep right on buying them. For if we can help end this war one day sooner, if our efforts can save the life of a single American boy, who can say that any sacrifice we can make is too great.

(OPENING COMMERCIAL)

And now, Ted, what's new?

(NEWS)

(SECOND COMMERCIAL)

Yesterday from the moment of darkness when the first news flashed in, and the lights and radios winked on in home after home across America as the news spread and took fire, and then through the dawn's early light there arose through the hearts of the people of our country a mighty chorus, a chorus of hopes and prayers, a chorus our boys must hear today. Because they were on the march at last; under the staccato of the news you can hear the steady trampling of their marching feet. And every minute of the day through our hearts and heads rang once more the deathless words of our greatest martial hymn of all, electrified with new meaning, the unconquerable spirit of our greatest crusade.

> MINE EYES HAVE SEEN THE GLORY OF THE COMING
>   OF THE LORD
> HE IS TRAMPLING OUT THE VINTAGE WHERE THE GRAPES
>   OF WRATH ARE STORED
> HE HATH LOOSED THE FATEFUL LIGHTNING OF HIS
>   TERRIBLE SWIFT SWORD
> HIS TRUTH IS MARCHING ON
>
> I HAVE SEEN HIM IN THE WATCH-FIRES OF A HUNDRED
>   CIRCLING CAMPS
> THEY HAVE BUILDED HIM AN ALTAR IN THE EVENING

DEWS AND DAMPS
I CAN READ HIS RIGHTEOUS SENTENCE BY DIM AND
    FLARING LAMPS
HIS DAY IS MARCHING ON

I HAVE READ A FIERY GOSPEL WRIT IN BURNISHED
    ROWS OF STEEL
AS YE DEAL WITH MY CONTEMPNERS, SO WITH YOU
    MY GRACE SHALL DEAL
LET THE HERO BORN OF WOMAN, CRUSH THE SERPENT
    WITH HIS HEEL
SINCE GOD IS MARCHING ON.

HE HAS SOUNDED FORTH THE TRUMPET THAT SHALL
    NEVER CALL RETREAT
HE IS SIFTING OUT THE HEARTS OF MEN BEFORE HIS
    JUDGMENT SEAT
OH, BE SWIFT MY SOUL TO ANSWER HIM, BE JUBILANT
    MY FEET
OUR GOD IS MARCHING ON.

IN THE BEAUTY OF THE LILIES, CHRIST WAS BORN
    ACROSS THE SEA
WITH A GLORY IN HIS BOSOM, THAT TRANSFIGURES
    YOU AND ME
AS HE DIED TO MAKE MEN HOLY, LET US DIE TO MAKE
    MEN FREE
WHILE GOD IS MARCHING ON.

That was written more than eighty years ago by Mrs. Julia Ward Howe, but everybody still knows these powerful words. It was written at the time of the Civil War when there was anger between the states of the North and South. Those angers are gone. There is only one Republic, only one battle hymn. And when before too long now, American armies march into Berlin and Tokyo, there will be bands playing "The Battle Hymn of the Republic" and men from the South, North, West, and East will be keeping step with the music.

Thanks for listenin.' And remember: if you don't write, you're wrong. Good-bye, folks!

Kate sits amidst a parcel of mail from listeners, circa 1941.

KATE SMITH SPEAKS — THURSDAY, JULY 13, 1944

Hello, everybody! To us at home, there's nothing more important than those requests we get now and then from our men at the front. As far as we're concerned, they are commands that must be fulfilled. A friend of mine was telling me the other day about the trouble she had had trying to fill a request from her soldier husband. The serviceman had broken his spectacles and had written her in a frenzy to have some lenses ground from his regular prescription and sent immediately to him. It involved quite a lot of trouble, and even when she got them off she couldn't be sure they'd reach him unbroken. If any of you who listen are having a similar experience, you'll be glad to know that we have facilities now in all theatres of war for furnishing and repairing eyeglasses for soldiers. All who need glasses are given two pairs from the Army, and these can be replaced promptly by military optical shops or the new portable repair shops which tour the field.

So if that soldier of yours happens to wear glasses, you needn't worry about him. He's getting the best of care and attention from the Army.

(OPENING COMMERCIAL)

And now, Ted, what's new?

(NEWS)

(CLOSING COMMERCIAL)

There is a mood to summer days—have you noticed? Morning is a splendid thing; morning rises, throwing a golden cape across all the universe in sight, and the sky is vivid blue and full of promise, and the air is clean and crisped with dew and something that you want to drink deep inside you. Morning is a challenge! In the morning you say "today, I will do this and this and this. Today I will accomplish something!" Morning is an inspiration. In the morning, the world is something you want to stretch out your arms to, and draw it in close. Morning is a singing thing: birds sing, water sings, wind sings, and the housewife sings at her work, with her doors and windows wide open to let the morning in.

There is a mood to summer days: noon is a drowsy thing. There is quiet to noons, have you noticed? Noon is the most silent time of the whole day. The trees seem weighted with silence; the birds that chattered an hour or two before give only an occasional contented twitter, and any winds that move go about on tiptoe. Noon is a silent time: a time for serious thought, for contemplation. For some, it is the prelude to sleep. For everyone, it is an interlude between morning and afternoon. You don't do much at noon. You think about what you've done, or what you're going to do. Noon is a peaceful thing. It's like a hand that rests for a moment in benediction. A calm and lovely thing.

Yes, there is a mood to summer days. Nights are gallant things; nights are clear and sweet and brave with stars, and rich with a beauty that catches at your heart. Nights are a thing of moonlight on trees, on flowers, on water. Nights are sheer magic, when all the fantasies the poets ever put to verse suddenly seem possible and close at hand. Puck and Oberon, Peter Pan, Thumbelina, Cinderella: all seem more real in the magic of a summer's night than anything mortal. Nights are fairy tales in summer: almost unbelievable in their beauty, and completely unforgettable.

Yes, there is a mood to summer days. Have you noticed? These are the country's lush days, of fullest beauty. These are the days you remember all through the year.

Thanks for listenin.' And remember, if you don't write, you're wrong. Good-bye, folks!

Kate advertised Post products, including Swans Down cake flour and Calumet baking powder. She said cheerily, "Being so fat and happy, I could sell any food product."

KATE SMITH SPEAKS —
MONDAY, AUGUST 14, 1944

Hello, everybody! Well, it could be worse, I guess. It might be 115 in the shade, instead of the present 95 degrees. And of course, it would be worse if we were all deprived of our electric fans and iced coffee and trips to the beach.

What I mean, naturally, is the weather. But the way it is right now is bad enough for me, and about 99 percent of the rest of the U.S.A. agrees with me. This entire nation has been in the grip of a prolonged heat wave for days on end, with many sections baked to a crisp.

What's more, there seems to be little relief in sight, especially for the folks along the East Coast. The weather bureau says this noon that a mass of cool air is moving eastward to provide the north central states with some relief, but by the time that breeze reaches New York it will be nothing but hot air. And the only rain in sight is a few scattered thundershowers, which won't mean much to the drought-stricken crops.

Here's my suggestion for today! Save up a couple of these August days, and put them in a safe-deposit box until next January. I for one would enjoy a little less of this right now, and a little more of it next winter.

(OPENING COMMERCIAL)

And now, Ted, what's new?

(NEWS)

Well, today we learn that spinach is not quite all it's cracked up to be. In fact, we are told now that a dish of spinach may well destroy the benefits derived from some other foods, for Popeye's favorite vegetable contains too much oxalic acid, a substance that interferes with the assimilation of calcium. Most people don't get enough calcium anyway, and eating too much spinach can cut down that quota even lower.

The nutritionists would like to ease spinach slightly out of the picture. They urge us to substitute broccoli, kale, lettuce, and collards, as these are rich in vitamins and contain less of the undesirable oxalic acid.

Yes, that announcement from the Agriculture Department contains some radical advice on the sometimes difficult subject of spinach. But I'm sure that thousands of American mothers wish that experts had answered one more suggestion: after all these years of struggling to get spinach down our throats, how are we going to have any easier time of it with kale and collard greens?

(CLOSING COMMERCIAL)

To keep the faith! Perhaps that is the most difficult thing we here on the home front have to do in these long months of war. It is necessary that we keep the faith; that we believe in our country and our countrymen. And yet sometimes as we read our papers and listen to our radio, our courage is shaken, we become cynical, and our faith in the future waivers. We wonder unhappily just what sort of a nation we are. We read of strikes; we hear of money-made individuals who will sacrifice everything for profits in dollars and cents. Certain people loaf on the jobs they hold in vital war industries. We have, perhaps, neighbors who patronize black markets for beef. We see, every day, big cars rolling along the highways; cars we know must be running on ill-gotten gas. There are those in our midst who are unconsciously attempting to defeat Democracy by holding prejudices against certain groups and nationalities; those in our midst who do not seem to care particularly what happens after our victory is won. We see people who are aiding inflation by spending large sums of money for extravagant luxuries. And we ask ourselves, in perplexity, what sort of people are we anyway? Are we as a nation worth the bloodshed and the sacrifice of those brave Americans who fight our battles on some alien soil? We ask ourselves these things, and our hearts grow faint with doubt and discouragement. But what we forget is the millions upon millions of upright, patriotic Americans in every city and town across this broad land who are working day and night for our cause; who are observing all the rules and doing the utmost to conserve supplies, and assure materials and arms for our fighting forces. Always, there are those who manage to shift the load on the shoulders of others. Always, there are those who enjoy the fruit of the honest labor of others. But, don't forget, I said a small minority. In that fact lies the sustenance for our faith in the future. For every individual who fails in his responsibility, there are thousands, perhaps hundreds of thousands, who carry more than their share of the burden. For them, let us keep the faith, each doing our part as best we can, with courage and dignity, unswerving in duty and loyalty—a constant example to that small minority who willfully deny themselves a share in the glory that comes with work and sacrifice, who cannot know the satisfaction of saying, "I have done my best. I have not been found wanting. I have kept the faith!"

Thanks for listenin.' And remember, if you don't write, you're wrong. Good-bye, folks!

Ted Collins was Kate's equal partner in business: the Kated Corporation. On each broadcast, at roughly 12:05, Kate asked, "And now, Ted, what's new? and he read several news items.

KATE SMITH SPEAKS — MONDAY, JANUARY 1, 1945

Hello, everybody! Today, as we begin the New Year of 1945, I want to extend to you all the very best wishes of us all: Ted Collins, the makers of Swansdown and Calumet, and myself! It seems to me the usual casual Happy New Year greeting is a bit out of tune with our times. Perhaps a far better wish, one nearer to our heart's desire, is a happier New Year, a victorious New Year, for only with victory and peace shall we again have it in our hearts to say Happy New Year. Let's hope and pray that one year from today we'll be using the old familiar New Year salutation, and our world will be restored to its lovely familiar pattern. Meantime, looking around the nation we see that in many ways this is a traditional New Year's Day. There may not be a turkey in every oven (laughing) or a chicken in every pot, but around the nation today in homes, clubs, canteens, and charitable and patriotic organizations, holiday dinners are being served. Friendly good cheer and kindness to the lonely and the poor are the order of the day. Down in Dallas, Texas, crowds are gathering for the football game in the Cotton Bowl, New Orleans' Sugar Bowl game will have many spectators who are disabled veterans of this war, thanks to the Young Men's Club there, and in Los Angeles, the Rose Bowl Game will take place as always. In factories and war plants some will be working, some will be absent. In Philadelphia, the Mummers will march according to custom. Yes, it's New Year's Day in wartime. Over in Brooklyn the Red Cross will keep its doors open for those who offer the gift of precious blood, so urgently needed. That's the picture on this holiday: work and play, a holiday mood, but tempered with the thought of war, and those who are absent, fighting our battles.

(FIRST COMMERCIAL)

And now, according to custom, shall we look back over the year of 1944: a year of pain and defeat, a year of brilliant victories, a year of splendid courage, and world-shaking events. 1944 will go down in history as the nation's third year in the second World War, but the year in which America laid the groundwork for peace. It will go down as the momentous year of decision, when the nation decided to take the lead in forming a world organization to prevent war. It was also the year in which the nation made a historic decision in the first wartime Presidential election since the Civil War. That election was the biggest national news, for the first man ever to win a third term won a fourth. 1944 was the year of conferences looking toward the future: Dumbarton Oaks, Bretton Woods, the Chicago Conference on International Aviation.

It was the year of heroes! The year of outstanding courage in kids like Private Saul Leavitt from Brooklyn, Don Gantile of Piqua, Ohio, Richard Bong of Poplar, Wisconsin, and Corporal Paul Huff, paratrooper, from the Tennessee Mountains. Yes, the year of heroes whose names are legion, fliers, sailors, foot-soldiers, and tough Marines from little towns across the land. It was the year of brave, patient women in uniform toiling silently in odd corners of a battle-scarred world. Here at home it was a year of war against inflation, black markets, and rumors. The pattern of industry was the same as in 1943; problems of production and manpower, problems of demand and supply, problems of strikes, and government seizures. It was a year of huge losses on the battle fronts, and yet it was a year of great gains, great advances. Above all in the headlines was the day that shook the world: Invasion Day, forged into our consciousness in letters of fire; the day of reckoning, marking the beginning of the downfall of Nazi Germany and the downfall of all who sanctioned and aided the black reign of terror and destruction that is Hitlerism. 1944 was a year when two great Americans, a man named Patton and a man named MacArthur, gave the lie to the Nazi accusation that the nation was soft and weak, and when millions of unnamed American lads proved how strong, how brave, how magnificent, are the men and women whose roots are in this soil. It was a year of bond buying, a year of grand books like "Your Kids and Mine," "My Country," "Brave

Men." There was grief in the nation over the loss of Al Smith and Wendell Willkie, and the loss of the silent legions whose graves are white crosses on some alien earth.

A year of big smashing events, and little things like women standing on line for butter, women carrying bundles, doing a major bookkeeping job with ration points, learning new recipes to patch up the food shortages. A year in which somehow housewives managed to keep the home-fires burning and the family well-fed and well-clothed despite scarcities. The songs of the nation went sentimental and slow, songs like "I'll Walk Alone," "Day After Forever," "It Could Happen To You," "Goodnight, Wherever You Are." And "Going My Way" walked off with the movie honors, while Barry Fitzgerald stole the picture as the old priest.

A nation was all out for war, and yet we had time for little things like writing V-mail letters and strolling in the park, taking the children to school, and planting the flowers of spring. Even in war, there is still the sun and the moon, the wind and the steadfast stars. The benediction of the first snowfall of winter, the lift in the first kiss of springtime on the hills of America, the quiet tiptoe of sunrise, the blazing splendor of the sky when the sun goes down at twilight.

These lovely simple things are still our own. These things we have not lost. We have lost much in the year just passed, but we have not lost the permanent things; things like the treasure of our ideals, the will and determination of men to be free, the will to make a better world out of the ashes of war and destruction and despotism. We have not lost the unity that makes willingness to sacrifice to make our dreams come true. We can hope and pray that in this year victory will be ours and peace restored to the tired world, but however long the struggle, however bitter the conflict, we can strive for dignity and stature and poise, as individuals and as a nation. We can strive to develop a nobility that will leave our imprint in timeless glory on this world, to be adequate, to hold steady and firm to the changeless values, and hold the lamp of faith high!

That is my New Year's wish to you; my wish for America: victory and peace, achieved by physical and spiritual strength. Let us remember these things as we go forward together in this year of 1945, sure of our cause, sure that a new day will dawn, pouring the dazzling sunlight of liberty and tranquility over a liberated earth.

And now, I see it's time for me to be on my way. My thoughts and my earnest prayers reach out to our men and women overseas, wherever they may be; prayers for their comfort and safety. My prayers reach out, too, to all of you who are lonely or sad, who have dear ones far away. May you soon be reunited and may all of us, everywhere, find in 1945 a happier New Year! Thanks for listenin' and remember, if you don't write, you're wrong. Good-bye, folks!

Kate listens as Ted reads "what's new" at their Camp Sunshine Studio.

KATE SMITH SPEAKS — FRIDAY, JANUARY 5, 1945

Hello, everybody! One of the most interesting Christian legends we have is that connected with this date, January 5th, for it is the Eve of Twelfth Night. It is related that when the Three Wise Men of the East were on their way to Bethlehem from Jerusalem, they passed an old woman cleaning her house. She asked them where they were going, and when they told her, she begged them to wait until she had finished her work, and she would go with them. The Wise Men replied they could not wait, but advised her to follow them. And so, when all her many tasks were done, she started, but they were out of sight. Ever since that day, according to the legend, she has been wandering about the world seeking the child Jesus. According to folklore of Russia and Italy, she goes down the chimneys of houses on the Eve of Twelfth Night, leaving gifts for children in the hope that at last she may find the blessed child whom she is seeking. There is little time in these hurried days to think of these ancient legends that have come down through the centuries, but it is good to pause and reflect on them now and then.

(FIRST COMMERCIAL)

We're all excited this morning over a little bit of a girl who's just come to town especially to appear on our Kate Smith Hour on Sunday. Her name is Margaret O'Brien. She's eight years old, and she bears none of the earmarks of a child prodigy. Margaret is a born actress, that's all! In other words, she's a normal youngster who likes to play with dolls, look at picture books, or skip rope like any other child her age. In her brief life so far, she's appeared in nine pictures. She was five years old when she won hearts by the million in that lovely movie "Journey for Margaret," and in her latest pictures, "Music for Millions" and "Meet Me in St. Louis," she's due to win more hearts. She doesn't dance, or sing, or play any musical instrument; with Margaret it's dramatic acting, so we know she'll give a wonderful performance on our Sunday Kate Smith Hour. We'll have other guests of course, too: our old friends Nan Ray and Mrs. Waterfall, Jackie Gleason, comedian from the current play "Follow the Girls," Woody Herman and his clarinet, and lots of other surprises.

So don't forget, make a note on your new calendar right now! You have a date with little Margaret O'Brien, Woody Herman, Jackie Gleason, Nan Ray and Mrs. Waterfall, me, and all the rest of our crowd. That's Sunday, at family get-together time, for the Kate Smith Hour: 7:00 p.m. Eastern Wartime.

And now, Ted, what's new?

(NEWS)

(SECOND COMMERCIAL)

Well, the fellow they call "Mister Frost" is trying to shake hands with everybody in town today. There isn't a white nose in view, and this Frost individual is writing his autograph on all windows on both sides of the street. Cold is what they call it in the weather communiqués, and increasingly cold at that.

This is the kind of weather that sets me dreaming of a red-glowing country-store coal stove; one of those pumpkin-shaped heaters with a shelf near the bottom for the shoe that hides a cold foot, with a flat surface on top for an emergency kettle of water.

The name of the stove I'm thinking of is "Pot Belly," and it stands inside a ramshackle wooden frame building.

Around my favorite stove in weather as sharp as this, there is nearly always a circle-like regularity throughout the day and early evening, and perhaps very late at night a few stragglers will huddle near the warmth-shedding old hunk of metal. Just through the doors on either side of this stove the wind bites deep and paints the ears fiery-red in five minutes. Only the brave and well bundled leave it to stand in the wind outside.

This stove draws man and boy, woman and girl, young and old, rich and poor, black and white, all creeds, all kinds. This stove is democratic. It warms everybody. There isn't so much gossip around it as you might expect. A man is likely to start up a conversation with the fellow next to him, but usually there isn't much said around the stove that stands in the ramshackle building. Folks seem to stick to their own knitting and respect the silence of others.

This old-fashioned country-store stove, where is it, you say? Out in the country a hundred miles from New York? Somewhere in the back hills of Vermont? Hidden in a New Hampshire valley? Oh, no. It's just down the street a few blocks from where I am. Right in the heart of old New York. Every elevated railway station waiting room on Third Avenue has one just like it. And now, Ted, what's new?

(NEWS)

Today, we salute young Harvard Merrill Hodgkins of Hancock Point, Maine. Harvard is the seventeen-year-old lad who aided in the capture of the two Nazi spies who landed on our shores near Bar Harbor, Maine. It's good Americans like this young man who are helping us to win the war against the most treacherous of enemies.

You know, many of us have been a little lax during the past few months. We've been too sure of ourselves. It might be well to take a lesson from young Hodgkins, keep our eyes open, and report anything suspicious to the authorities. Nobody knows how many other Nazi German and Japanese spies may be operating in our midst. Mr. J. Edgar Hoover has mentioned two Japanese balloons:

one found last Sunday near Portland, Oregon, the other three weeks ago in Montana. There may be others. Whether they contained spies or explosives is not known. If they carried spies, such spies may be Germans rather than Japanese, since it is less easy for us to spot a German than a Japanese.

May I remind you again that we are fighting a determined and clever enemy who will stop at nothing to get within our gates for his own evil purpose? It is important, more vital now than ever, that we refrain from talking about troop movements, ships' names, war plant production or any other information concerning war when we are in a public place. Also bear in mind that we must all keep on the alert, and report at once to the nearest FBI office any suspicious activities or any suspicious characters who are strangers in our community. That's one way we at home can help our fighting forces.

Thanks for listenin,' and remember: if you don't write, you're wrong. Good-bye, folks!

KATE SMITH SPEAKS —
TUESDAY, JANUARY 30TH, 1945

Hello, everybody! Today there is cause for triple celebration on our President's part. It's the date of the Inauguration Ball, the climax of the March of Dimes campaign, and it's Mr. Roosevelt's birthday.

Yes, our President is sixty-three years old today, but although birthdays mean parties in most families, Mr. Roosevelt is far too busy to observe this anniversary with any ceremony.

Of far more importance is the big task of winning the war, and those problems cannot be delayed even one day for birthday cake and candles. While the rest of the nation celebrates the Inauguration and the March of Dimes parties and sends a hearty congratulation to Mr. Roosevelt on his sixty-third birthday, the President himself will take no public part in his anniversary observance.

(FIRST COMMERCIAL)

And now, Ted, what's new?

(NEWS)

With so many world-shaking events filling the news of each day, the significance of special dates on the calendar is sometimes overlooked by many of us. Just as a refresher on today's date, let me remind you that it was just twelve years ago today that Hitler was named Chancellor of the Reich. It was on the same date four years later in 1937 that the same Hitler made a bombastic speech saying that Germany annulled and repudiated any responsibility for the first World War. It was on January 30, 1943 that the RAF bombed Berlin twice during the Nazi rally celebrating the tenth anniversary of their rise to power.

Yes, this date of January 30th has been significant for Hitler and his Nazi gangsters in the past. Only the future can disclose what this date in the years to come may mean to the brief and inglorious star of Nazi Germany. But with our armies and the armies of our Allies pressing ever steadily closer and closer to the heart of the Nazi capital, Berlin itself, we who know the nature of our enemies and who can never forget their atrocious record of blood-shed, murder, and destruction, can hope and pray that when another January 30th rolls around there will be no cause for celebration in Germany; that fascism will be shorn of its power once and for all and the guilty will be punished according to the crimes they have committed against the civilized world.

(SECOND COMMERCIAL)

Not long ago, in one of our daily newspapers, there was a cartoon which amused me very much. It showed two GIs beside their foxhole. One was sitting and reading a clipping sent in a letter from home, a clipping all about postwar plans for veterans, and the soldier who was reading was saying he didn't want a job—he wanted a rest! I smiled to myself at the time, but there's a more serious side to this business of our returning servicemen.

It seems to be the impression of a good many people that when our millions of fighting men come back, they'll be a tremendous problem; that the war will have changed them considerably, that they'll be in a class apart. Jobs will have to be gotten for them, decisions will have to be made for them, and they'll find life in the USA exceedingly difficult. I do not hold to this opinion at all. Our soldiers, sailors, and marines want to get the job they're doing now over with as quickly as possible. They want to win the victory and return to civilian life. Except for the military experience they've gained during their stretch in combat, they're no different from any other Americans. They long for a chance to think for themselves again, to be individuals, to get back to their homes and their farms and their trades. Even those who are partially disabled will not want those on the home-front to regard them as helpless. They want to exercise their own thinking processes, have a voice in politics, complain a little if they feel so inclined, become a part of their own town again, and their own church, and their own community. In short, they want to slip back into their old familiar places and exercise their individual rights to do and think as they please, just as they did before they went away. Some of them, it is true, may want to strike out in a different city or a different state where they've found wider horizons and greater opportunities. But mostly, I think they'll want to come home and stay home, and not be regarded in their communities as strange creatures who'll never, never be the same again.

All of us agree, of course, that they must have as much encouragement and help and benefits as they want and need. But to my way of thinking the best way that they can be helped most and the way they themselves will prefer, is to come back to a prosperous America with industry in all its branches going full tilt. Economic security is one thing, but economic opportunity is far more important. It has been the goal of free people since America's very beginning. Let each and every one of us keep it that way and do our utmost to retain that familiar title our forefathers gave it—not the land of security—but the blessed "Land of Opportunity."

Thanks for listenin' and remember: if you don't write, you're wrong. Goodbye, folks!

KATE SMITH SPEAKS —
FRIDAY, APRIL 13, 1945

The President died yesterday afternoon at Warm Springs, Georgia. The nation mourns the only President the U.S. has known since 1933. Note that today is Friday the 13th.

Hello, everybody!

Out in Missouri, in the heart of our great country, a very old lady is praying this noon.

She's 92 and she's a mother. She's praying because her son has just taken over the world's biggest and greatest job. She's Mrs. Martha Truman, mother of the President of these United States.

"We are praying," she said, "that God will guide him."

I think the rest of the nation might well join in that prayer.

And now, Ted, what's new?

(NEWS)

During the past eighteen anguished hours, you have heard through your radios and read in your newspapers many eloquent tributes to Mr. Franklin Delano Roosevelt, guiding light of this great nation, known to all of us simply as Mr. Roosevelt, or Mr. President. Let this tribute of mine be simple. Let it be little words straight from the heart at the passing of a friend, as well as a leader among men.

For in the beginning, there was no fanfare, no drum rolls, no oratory. There was just a little American boy, growing. A little American boy playing like other American boys, with abandon; skinning his nose, wearing holes through his shoes, planning to run away to sea. He always loved the sea and the sailing ships. His mind always reached out to far places and brave adventures. Strangely, and in jest, destiny spoke to him when he was a lad of five. With his mother, he was meeting for the first time a President of the United States, President Grover Cleveland, and the great statesman looked at the youngster, Franklin, and greeted him with these words: "I'll give you a wish to remember for the rest of your life, young fellow: Pray to God that he never lets you become President of the United States."

The boy forgot those words as soon as he heard them but his mother carried them in her heart for the rest of her life, and Destiny must have been listening and smiling triumphantly then. And so, he grew from short trousers to long as other boys had grown before him. He studied, he played pranks, he was graduated with honors and won the all-school Latin prize, a prize that meant less to him than the record he established for the running high kick. He went to college; Harvard claimed him as its own. He fell in love and married his cousin, Anna Eleanor. They lived in a small house in New York and he became associated with a law firm; a simple pattern, a direct pattern, an American pattern. It would always remain an American pattern, but already Destiny was reaching out to the young man who had grown up at Hyde Park. The people wanted him for their candidate for the State Senatorship. That was the beginning of greatness, the beginning of his loss of privacy. Henceforth he would be a public servant; history groomed him as she saw fit.

He was Assistant Secretary of the Navy during the first World War. He ran for Vice President on the ticket with Cox and knew defeat. Yet his life was full and active and busy. He lived close to the sea whenever he could. He enjoyed sailing; took long walks in the woods with his sons. And then the Fates that had given him health and the joy of living, snatched health away. He was stricken with the dread affliction, infantile paralysis. He who had strode the country lanes, had stood at the tiller with the wind in his face, was to know these things no longer except in his memories. For three years Franklin Delano Roosevelt fought to move, fought to live, and in those years he learned much, as all who die a living death must learn. And his suffering left him older and wiser, more tolerant. Then he was taken to Warm Springs, and after a year had passed, he knew the joy of walking again with the help of a cane: walking slowly, painfully, but walking! It was then that his dream began, the dream of a foundation that would make it possible to help others afflicted with infantile paralysis. Later, at the urging of his friends, he consented to run on the Democratic ticket for Governor of New York state. He had but one more step to go to become a leader of men.

It was in March 1933 that he began his duties in the White House, and even then, long before the beating of the drums of war, he was weighed down with responsibilities. Remember those days? The banks had closed; there were breadlines; men and women shivered on street corners selling apples. Depression and want stalked across the land that was America. America, land of promise, land of plenty, almost without hope in those heartbreaking days of 1933, apathetic, questioning, doubtful—afraid! And the new President spoke and said: "The only thing we have to fear is fear itself." Depression did not vanish overnight, but there was new life in the nation, new spirit in the Capitol. The banks were re-opened, the farmers were aided, money was put into circulation. The man who had faith in America, gave America back faith in herself. And all the time the mounting shadow grew across the seas, the shadow of war. He knew no such thing as isolation, knew that America could not escape, but he loved peace, just as all Americans love peace. For a time he tried to fight to build up the Army, the Navy. He was criticized, his policies were attacked, but there were few among the millions who ever questioned his sincerity of purpose, his deep, abiding zeal for America, and at the time he was elected to a third term, he received the greatest tribute of confidence that could come to any man.

There's no need to repeat the annals of his greatness when war did engulf us, or his magnificent leadership through those dark days when we were stunned and horrified by the suddenness of the lightning bolt in the Pacific. You all know these things, for it was then, in the midst of our common peril, that all of us, from the man in the street, from the bootblack to the grocer to the banker, to the leaders of our Allies, began really to know Franklin D. Roosevelt, for all the world listened to him, and leaned on him. Thus came the burdens that proved too heavy to bear: work, and travel to the far corners of the earth. Worry, loneliness, problems, big tall thoughts in the stillness of the long night; responsibilities of a magnitude few of us can even understand became part and parcel of the life of this one man. Freedom of Speech—that freedom of speech that Americans delight in—hurled accusations at him, doubted him, questioned him, but never doubted his sincerity of purpose, never doubted that he was giving his life in his country's cause. We all knew he must falter and some day fall; we all knew his physical health was growing weaker and weaker, and yet when we heard his cheerful, confident voice over the radio, when he imbued us with his courage, we forgot the iron braces and the wheel-chairs. We forgot the strained look on the face of the man aged too soon by the responsibilities of war. He was a simple man. I think I remember him best as he was in those good days before war cast its blight on the world. I remember him as he was that evening in the White House when the King and Queen of England were there and I had been invited to sing some of his favorite songs and some of theirs. And there, even in the presence of royalty, he was outstanding in his graceful manners, his dignity, his genial informal courtesy, his magnetic personality that won admirers and friends for him even among those who disagreed with his political beliefs. Yes, I remember him best as he was on that evening when I stood there and sang simple American songs for the illustrious group gathered in that room. And singing, I watched his face and saw him smile, and when the songs were done, he applauded heartily and thanked me, saying he loved the old songs best. That evening is something pretty special to press between the memory pages of my heart, and though I saw him many times after that, they were serious times when there was no singing of old songs but only talk of war and bonds, and meetings in the far-flung corners of the earth.

And now he's gone. A great soul has passed beyond the care and the worry of this mortal world, and we who mourn his loss offer our prayers and our tears, and a nation is bereft. But there is a greater tribute than tears, greater than mourning. Let us, every American, man, woman, and child, wherever we are, at home in the United States or on the battlefronts of the world, offer the tribute of a high resolve. Let us pledge ourselves now to shoulder gloriously the burden he has had to lay down, to follow his leadership, to fight as he has fought: to keep faith as he has kept faith through those dark days that lie far behind us now. Let that be our tribute to Franklin Delano Roosevelt, outstanding leader and great American gentleman. May he who died in the midst of war rest, in peace!

Thanks for listenin' and good-bye, folks!

Many broadcasts were done at Kate's elegant Park Avenue apartment. Note the portrait above the fireplace.

KATE SMITH SPEAKS —
THURSDAY, APRIL 26, 1945

Hello, everybody! Well, if the American housewife needs any further reminder that this war is far from won, that continued care of her buying habits must be the order of the day until final victory, she has it this noon in the latest announcement of the office of Price Administration.

For beginning next Sunday and until further notice, she must make those precious red points do a bigger job than ever. All but one-half of one per cent of the nation's total meat supply will be brought under strict rationing controls in an effort to spread more evenly the civilian meat supply which will drop another six million pounds during May. The only type of meat still available without points will be mutton.

Other changes in the meat and fat rationing program for May will be increases of one to two points per pound for most cuts of lamb and veal and one point for most beef steaks; decreases of one to two points for beef roasts and other cuts of beef; increases of four points for margarine. And two points for grade-one cheese.

The expanded program for May puts meat rationing back where it was a year ago before most meats were made point-free. But OPA Chief Chester Bowles believes there should be improved distribution of existing supplies as a result of OPA's new meat control program.

(FIRST COMMERCIAL)

Remember that song of only a few seasons back? "I Got a Gal in Kalamazoo!" Well, those gals in that town seem to get into the news in one way or another now and then. Lately the girls at Kalamazoo College have been conducting a survey about post-war husbands and if that survey is any indication, the creature of their dreams must be just about perfect! Looks don't mean so much to them; in fact the dark-haired Romeos and the blue-eyed Prince Charmings are out! What they do want is a tall man who does not sport a mustache but has a good, sun-tanned complexion. He must not be a mother's boy, and must have enough character and gumption to "wear the pants" in the family. They'll let him have a temper, too, but he must be able to control it. Their ideal man must have a fondness for mystery stories, children, home cooking, and dogs! He must be faithful and affectionate; must let his wife wear slacks if she wants to, and he must also smoke a pipe! He must never sulk, must be intelligent but not obviously so, and he must be able to write interesting letters! But, gentlemen, if you've "Got a Gal in Kalamazoo" don't be discouraged; the song writer didn't sing of the charms of the Kalamazoo girls for nothing. Off the record, word has gotten around that a 100 percent compliance with all specifications is not expected!

And now, Ted, what's new?

(NEWS)

We hear a great deal these days about certain popular books that sell thousands and thousands of copies, but there's one book that tops all others. It's been the world's best seller for quite a while now, and still continues to be—by a wide margin. According to Dr. Daniel L. Marsh, President of Boston University, more than 33 million copies of the Holy Bible, or portions of it, were issued and sent throughout the world last year!

(SECOND COMMERCIAL)

This is the story of "Little Danny" Sullivan. It isn't much of a story because, you see, I never did know "Little Danny" and all I have of him is a ten-line story tucked away in the back pages of one of our New York newspapers. But if you read between the lines, you have an urge to speak to him, to pay one last tribute to him because he's lost and forgotten in the big headline news.

I don't suppose Danny Sullivan was ever headlined. I don't suppose he ever even received "billing" during the twelve years he worked as a clown with Ringling Brothers' Circus, for he was just a little fellow—he was only three feet ten inches tall. And yet in my mind's eye I can see him, putting on his grease paint, making himself a ridiculous red nose, capering about in baggy clothes, turning somersaults, and scampering about with one thought: to make the children laugh. That's the business of clowns: never to be sad, never to be quiet, never to think tall serious thoughts, but just to make people laugh. Danny probably wasn't much to look at; one of the little people who never did grow as other men did; one of the small, insignificant figures of life who could never achieve anything beyond making a ridiculous appearance and adding to the mirth and jollity of the greatest show on earth. And yet, "Little Danny" Sullivan, underneath the grease paint and the funny wig, underneath the tramp's costume that clowns so often wear, must have had a heart for something besides laughter, must have had a mind occupied with more serious contemplation than the antics of the Big Top. There was no obituary which eulogized him, but somehow I think there ought to be. For in the small news item I mentioned a moment ago there are these brief lines: "For the last two years he had been employed in a Kansas City airplane factory, where he was assigned to jobs in small compartments of planes inaccessible to larger employees." Little Danny Sullivan, erstwhile clown, died on that job. He died on April 21st, out there in Missouri. He wouldn't have been drafted; he was too small for that. But he took a war job—a war job that others couldn't do—he was big enough for that!

I guess it's something pretty special to have been able to bring the gift of laughter and light hearts to hundreds of thousands of people for twelve long years and then, when the need came, to switch to a job where there was no exciting circus. Danny took his final curtain call last Saturday. The little clown has gone. But I offer him the tribute of my applause today, for I think Daniel W.

Sullivan, known to the circus folks as "Little Danny," must have been quite a man though he was less than four feet tall!

Thanks for listenin' and remember, if you don't write, you're wrong! Good-bye, folks!

Kate conducted several radio war bond marathons and was responsible for the sale of some $600 million from pledges.

KATE SMITH SPEAKS —
MONDAY, APRIL 30TH, 1945

False rumors of victory in Europe.

Hello, everybody! Bitter disappointment settled over the face of America this weekend. Bitter because the four-year long hopes and prayers of a whole nation seemed answered, then the answer proved a cruel deception after all.

Shortly before 8 p.m. Saturday night radio stations across the country were interrupting programs to bring America the long-awaited news of peace in Europe.

In a matter of minutes, 50,000 people were filling New York's Times Square with jubilant shouts and cheers.

Those same minutes heard a solemnly joyous crowd in front of the White House singing "God Bless America" and "The Star Spangled Banner."

Those minutes saw Chicago newspapers turning out Victory Extras with banner headlines, based on the false Associated Press surrender report.

In Minneapolis, Atlanta, San Francisco—all over the United States—countless millions of mothers, wives, sisters, and sweethearts heard the words they had dreamed of for such a long time.

The heart of the nation was singing, but the song soon died. President Truman announced that we were still a nation at war. Peace had not come. The surrender report was an error.

Well, this is not time for bitterness and blame. The whole incident was most unfortunate; cruelly unfortunate. But let each of us keep in mind the White House announcement that when the news of German surrender is officially confirmed, the President will read the official proclamation over the air at once.

So until President Truman tells us that peace has come to Europe, let's keep ourselves dedicated to the business of winning the war on the home front.

(FIRST COMMERCIAL)

Spring cleaning is underway these days all over the country. In the tiniest house by the side of the road and the great mansions of the rich, the vacuum cleaners are humming. The soap-suds are flying, and women are going to town with mop and broom. And the White House in Washington is no exception. Spring cleaning came to the nation's number one house last week, and it's a big job. This is the first time in twelve years that it's been unoccupied, and right now painters and decorators have taken over to make everything spic and span for President Truman and his family when they move in on May 1st.

Mrs. Henrietta Nesbitt, the housekeeper, is on hand to see that the White House gets a cleaning job deluxe, and Mrs. Truman, our new First Lady, is supervising the decorating of the family quarters. When you consider that the buildings and grounds cover an area of 16 acres, and that the main building is four stories high, with east and west wings which in themselves are some 215 feet long and 35 feet wide, you can imagine that spring cleaning at the White House is a major operation! And if you get to thinking of the work involved, well, maybe it isn't so bad to be living in your own little home with three or four rooms and bath!

And now, Ted, what's new?

(NEWS)

(SECOND COMMERCIAL)

April is traditionally the month of spring, when grass turns green, the leaves unfold, and the world begins to live again after the bleakness of winter. But this year, April also brought death; death to two men known the world over—one as the leader of a great democracy, the other as a dictator and tyrant.

The first, Franklin Delano Roosevelt, lies at Hyde Park, his grave a shrine to millions of American people of today, and Americans to come. Franklin Delano Roosevelt died in honor, revered and loved by the people.

The body of the other man lies battered, dirty, disgraced, in the center of Milan, Italy. Yes, Benito Mussolini, the "Balcony Dictator," is dead, shot by his own people, hated, scorned, and spat upon, even in death.

He was caught as he attempted to flee to Switzerland, huddled in a German military overcoat to escape detection. When he was arrested by the Italian patriots, he was "shocked," for he thought these patriots whom he had flogged and beaten for twenty-six years had come to free him.

He was given a trial and found guilty. And an hour later, Mussolini, with sixteen of his fascist henchmen, were lined up against the wall and shot. His sixteen friends died bravely, but Mussolini, his bravado gone, fell pleading and promising to trade an empire he did not have, for his life.

It was considered ironic justice that the mortal remains of the fascist dictator be taken for all to see to Milan, where his black-shirted fascism was born twenty-six years ago.

By that time Mussolini, son of a country village blacksmith, already had seen a varied career as a soldier, socialist, editor, and teacher.

In 1919, he formed the first "fasci" and first was called "Il Duce." And by 1922, he had a million followers who declared that if the Italian government were not given them, they would take it. The frightened little Italian King at last invited the barrel-chested blacksmith's son to form a cabinet, and the colorful, swaggering, brutal career of Mussolini was on its way.

The first of the modern dictators at one time treated Adolf Hitler as something of a pupil, but the "master" was soon outstripped in brutality and crime. And when the Axis partnership was formed, Mussolini was the junior member.

When our troops invaded Sicily, he knew his game was up, and he fled to the protection of his compatriot Hitler, as a beaten, broken man.

On April 12, 1945, the world mourned Franklin Roosevelt. From Cedar Rapids, Iowa, to Chungking, China, the peoples of the world wept, unashamed, for their loss.

But on April 29, 1945, there were no tears for Benito Mussolini. Italy rejoiced. I say, "good riddance."

Thanks for listenin' and remember: if you don't write, you're wrong! Good-bye, folks!

KATE SMITH SPEAKS —
TUESDAY, AUGUST 14TH, 1945

Hello everybody! This, perhaps, is the day we've waited three years, eight months and seven days for.

Today, August 14th, 1945, looks very much like the last day of the war with Japan. The last bomb of World War II may have fallen. The last life may have been given for freedom's sake, for today may be V-J Day. If Japan's reply does come through to the White House today, and if the Presidential proclamation is forthcoming, then this most surely is it.

But, we must remember that the false alarms and trigger flashes of the past three days may be repeated for the next few hours. And it could be some time before the final end to all our waiting is announced. That is why the mounting tide of joy that is rising over the world at this moment carries an undercurrent of sobering thought. There's a world-wide celebration under way this noon, but the participants are held back just a little by a caution born of skepticism. Until the President makes the peace official, there's always room for doubt.

All the cities of America, and most others throughout the world, with the outstanding exception of Tokyo, are cheering the victory right now. But the celebrations in most cities are tame compared with the uncontrolled exhilaration that swept this country in 1918. The news that Japan is ready for surrender unconditionally brought Americans tumbling out of bed at 2 a.m., but they took it calmly and soberly. Instead of snake dancing in the streets, thousands of them are kneeling in prayer in the churches of the nation. Probably San Francisco's celebration is the largest. The news of Tokyo's surrender broadcast reached there just before eleven last night, while streets, restaurants, and night clubs were still filled. And of all the celebrants in that Pacific port of embarkation, the most joyous were thousands of servicemen who had been waiting for ships to take them into battle. A sailor climbed on a theater marquee and tossed down the letters from the sign, one by one. A navy Ensign swaggered down Market Street sporting a Colonel's cap. The whole town, while keeping a skeptical eye out for further developments, cut loose with the revelry they had saved over from a quiet V-E Day.

But across the country, the nation's largest city took the good news more calmly. New York City, the town of riotous demonstration, uninhibited revelry, and inflammable enthusiasm, indulged in a little tooting of auto horns and a little throwing of confetti. The crossroads of the world is jammed with thousands of celebrators who are singing and cheering in an orderly manner.

Washington is hardly more excited. The biggest crowd in town is the crowd gathered in Lafayette Park, just across from the White House. Those watchers are waiting for the word from the President that will turn them loose.

But it's in other parts of the world that the real, all-out celebrations are going on. The corner of the world that first felt the blows of Japan's military, Hawaii, Guam, and the Philippines, has become a melee of noise and fireworks. Every ship in Pearl Harbor was lighted from stem to stern for the first time since December 7th, 1941. And every soldier and sailor in those Pacific ports, far from home, is cutting loose with all the enthusiasm he has kept pent-up. Victory Day may mean a turning point in world affairs. For American servicemen overseas, it means the one thing they've waited for, and fought for, and dreamed of, for three long years: the time to go home.

This then, is V-J Day, 1945...perhaps? But remember only President Truman's final word can make it certain. Until then, we have a few more minutes, or hours, or days, to wait!

(OPENING COMMERCIAL)

And now, Ted, what's new?

(NEWS)

(CLOSING COMMERCIAL)

The end of the war won't come any too soon for one particular group of Americans.

That is the group of servicemen numbering some 15,000 sailors, soldiers, and Marines, now languishing in Jap prison camps.

Many have been there for more than three long years, living under the intolerable conditions that exist as a matter of course where Jap camps are concerned.

Most American prisoners were taken when Bataan fell in April, 1942. A month later, Corregidor gave in, and its surrender was followed shortly by that of American forces in the Southern Philippines.

It wasn't long after that we found out, through Tokyo radio, just how many prisoners the Japs had taken. An enemy broadcast said 25,000 American servicemen were then Jap captives.

But as the months went by the total slowly was whittled down.

Unfortunately, we ourselves had something to do with the loss of prisoner life.

At least three Jap ships carrying the American prisoners were sunk by American planes and submarines, with heavy casualties.

Then, too, the Japanese themselves reported that recent Superfort raids killed a number of prisoners held in the Jap home islands.

But countless other American deaths are attributed to vicious enemy negligence for the care of prisoners. Many died as a result of starvation, exposure, and sickness.

Authorities believe that loss of life among the prisoners was especially heavy last winter.

Last year, you will recall, the Japs transported more than 10,000 Americans from the tropical Philippines to Manchuria and Japan. All were undernourished, poorly-clothed. And there was no promise that these men would be given a greater allotment of clothing and food to withstand the rigors of winter farther north.

In any case, only time will tell just how the prisoners managed to survive the long years in Japanese hands. Let's pray that they have fared much better than we expect.

Thanks for listenin' and remember: if you don't write, you're wrong! Good-bye, folks!

Three military officers join Kate outside the Nation's Capitol in her home town.

(BROADCAST #2259)
KATE SMITH SPEAKS —
WEDNESDAY, AUGUST 15TH, 1945

The rumors were true. Yesterday was, indeed, V-J Day. The war was over!

Hello, everybody! Now, after years of agony, years of pain and heartbreak and endless waiting, we are at peace with the world and the world is at peace with us.

TED COLLINS:
It has been a long 44 months since Pearl Harbor. In those 44 months, thousands of American kids who left the football fields, the baseball lots, and the basketball courts have aged ten years. Some of them have looked death in the face so often they can't be kids any more, and the things they used to call dangerous won't make much of a dent on them in the future.

KATE SMITH:
Ted, I'll think of those 44 months as clusters of minutes and hours and days all strung together in a bad dream that wouldn't end. Time and tears, time and mud, time and the sound of news tickers beating out a story of war: the greatest and the worst story in history.

TED COLLINS:
Each of us knew one or two or maybe more boys who fought it and lived through it or fell fighting it, but few of us will ever know what it was really like. It's over and all the world was hurt by it and most of the world suffered up close to it. But we never heard a bomb down the block from our homes and we don't know the way some people know how it feels to have bullets and shells crashing into our homes in the dark of night.

KATE SMITH:
In years to come we will hear how it was for those who fought it through. Tongues of soldiers will someday loosen as time softens their memories of battle. Then we will know how it was.
But it may be a long time before we know.

TED COLLINS:
I'm thinking of a day 20 years from now when the veterans of this war are a little too stout to wear the old uniforms. I'm thinking of a day 20 years from now when the veterans hold their convention and stage their parade. I wonder if we'll be wise enough to remember, 20 years ahead, how much it cost us in human life and material resources to save the world from slavery. Will yet-unborn generations believe everything their fathers tell them of war, everything their history books say of war? Will they jump on war-makers before war-makers can seize control of nations? It's the biggest question civilization will have to answer.

KATE SMITH:
Sometime in the next 20 years the people of America, who have learned such wisdom as "see-your-dentist-twice-a-year" will have to learn to look into the hearts of troublemakers twice a year, not at a glance but by a searching look born of World War II.

TED COLLINS:
Days of peace, ways of peace. This is our new chance to prove that we are fit to exist as a people and a nation. By the will of a greater power than our own, by the deeds of the brave, and the intelligence of our commanders we have earned a new lease on life.

KATE SMITH:
GOD BLESS...THE DAWN OF PEACE!

(OPENING COMMERCIAL)

And now, Ted , what's new?

(NEWS)

(CLOSING COMMERCIAL)

The magic news that has transformed the entire world has brought forth from radios a steady stream of the events leading up to this moment of victory and peace. Millions of words have been spoken. I thank God that the fighting is over; that the enemy is vanquished. But this day, which will go down in history for those who come after us to read and to study, is only the beginning of the grave tasks that lie ahead. This chaotic world must be set in order, step by step. Millions must be fed and clothed; other millions, the enemies who no longer feel the impact of our physical might, must be taught an entirely new way of life: a philosophy which does not include aggression and cruelty and the absolute worship of a Hitler or a Hirohito. They must be taught that there is no super-race, that all men are equal and have an equal right to enjoy the fruits of this earth and the tranquility and decency to which the truly civilized subscribe. Surrender by Japan, for instance, does not necessarily mean that soldiers can get out of the army within six months. It does not mean that our responsibilities are over and that we will suddenly emerge into our pre-war status of a land of milk and honey. War exacts a high toll; we will be paying for war for many, many years. Only if mankind will war be worth the terrific price we've paid. We can't count on nylons for Christmas, or a sudden stoppage of food rationing, or an abundance of cars on the road, or a flood of the luxuries and conveniences we have missed since December 7th, 1941 and it seems to me, it is good that this is so. It's good that our mills and our factories will have to hum with peacetime projects to give industry a chance to catch up with consumer demand, for there will be millions of men and women who will need jobs. And so, on this blessed day of victory when our joy runs high, it is not too soon to give serious thought to the heroes we applaud on this day: the Americans who have won this war in the Pacific. What they need, and will continue to need in the years to come, is jobs, and security, and homes, and a decent way of life for themselves and their families. Some of them will need education. Thousands of others, alas, will need expert care and hospitalization. Let us all, every individual, community, town, city, and state lend every effort to this accomplishment. It's glorious to have flags flying, and drums of peace beating instead of drums of war. It's wonderful to know the shooting is over and Americans are going to come home instead of going overseas, but it is not too soon on this day of thanksgiving and prayer to think about what we can do for them, they who have done so much for us. They need more than lip-service. Let us, who await their return so eagerly, see that they get every consideration, every facility, every aid, every job that it is possible to give them. Let's keep on doing first things first!

Thanks for listenin' and remember: if you don't write, you're wrong (there are still many, many men far from home, looking for those letters from YOU)! Good-bye, folks!

Kate autographs a torpedo at the Navy submarine base in New London, Connecticut: 1942.

When the engineer gave the finger signal, Ted said, "It's high noon in New York and time for Kate Smith. Here she is." And she said, "Hello everybody."

Log Cabin syrup is poured onto waffles made for a recipe book.

Kate bakes, using Swans Down cake flour and Calumet baking powder.

III
THE POSTWAR ERA

1. FRIDAY, JUNE 28, 1946. Kate and Ted discuss summer camp for children. A doctor's ingenuity, of wiping out opium in Japan, and the final Kate Smith Hour of the season.

2. WEDNESDAY, AUGUST 28, 1946. Industrious Alaskans, "What's the use of wishing?"

3. MONDAY, DECEMBER 2, 1946. Ted has heart trouble and will be off the air for two months. Harry Marble and others will do the news reports.

4. MONDAY, FEBRUARY 24, 1947. The controversial broadcast about how racketeer Lucky Luciano got to Cuba.

5. WEDNESDAY, JUNE 4, 1947. A doll show, an editorial about teachers' salaries, and a home for the elderly.

6. FRIDAY, JUNE 20, 1947. Farewell to CBS, as final Kate Smith Speaks on that network.

7. MONDAY, JUNE 23, 1947. Hello to Mutual! Kate speaks of summer vacations in America, gives kudos to the Salt Lake City Safety Patrol.

8. MONDAY, AUGUST 11, 1947. Ted wishes he was at the Alabama Deep Sea Fishing Rodeo. Kate speaks of the old time tea wagon and of composer Carrie Jacobs Bonds.

9. TUESDAY, AUGUST 26, 1947. State fairs, a night-blooming primrose, a conference for silversmiths.

10. TUESDAY, JULY 13, 1948. Women and the housing shortage and at political conventions, Communism and religion.

11. THURSDAY, NOVEMBER 4, 1948. It's two days after Truman's surprise victory over Dewey and Kate urges Americans to write the President expressing their support.

12. THURSDAY, NOVEMBER 25, 1948. Ted offers his advice on carving the turkey while Kate speaks of Thanksgiving blessings.

13. FRIDAY, DECEMBER 31, 1948. Ways to spend New Year's Eve. Kate is listed among the Ten First Ladies of the World. She gives a New Year's message.

14. FRIDAY, MAY 6, 1949. The Kentucky Derby, quadruplets, older folks in the Bronx applying for jobs.

15. MONDAY, MAY 9, 1949. Is the White House to be replaced? Kate pleads for a man ill with tuberculosis to return home. Sunday is "I Am An American" Day.

KATE SMITH SPEAKS, FRIDAY, JUNE 28, 1946

Read the script as you listen to the program to see how closely they follow the script.

We think of this as a highly modern world but every day as I consider the things that are happening in this great country of ours, events we're beginning to take for granted what with all the shortages, it seems to me these times are reminiscent of our pioneer days in America They call for the same sort of ingenuity and determination that our forefathers had. Take the case of a doctor of Valley Stream, Long Island. He found out pretty quickly that a doctor home from the wars today, a veteran of World War II, doesn't come back to the practice he left when he went away. When he got his discharge from the Army last November and went home to Valley Stream, he took a rest, then decided to hang out his shingle again. That's when his troubles began. First, he had to find an office and a place to live; that took until April. Then, when he had a roof over his head and finally managed to get a telephone, he wondered how he'd answer calls, day or night, without a car. He couldn't get a car, so he did a lot of walking. Finally, he bought a bicycle. That's what he's using now to make his calls. He rides his rounds on the two-wheeler, pedaling his way up and down hills, around the countryside. He says he has his practice back again now, and he's going to keep it even if he has to get around on roller skates! His little story is not unusual today, but there's something inspiring about it. It makes me feel, together with all the other stories of ingenuity like it across the USA, that the pioneer spirit in America is very much alive! And I guess we'll keep it so, no matter what comes!

And now, Ted, what's new?

(NEWS)

And in the news behind the news, I saw a little item the other day that interested me more than all the atom bomb tests or reports of the United Nations. Did you see that item. Ted, about the good work our men have been doing in Japan to wipe out the traffic in opium?

TED COLLINS:

Yes, Kathryn, I did. It didn't make the headlines, but you're right about its importance. Colonel Crawford F. Sams, chief of public health and welfare in General Douglas MacArthur's headquarters, reported a few days ago that American occupation forces in Japan and Korea have cut off 90 percent of the world's pre-war illicit drug trade at its source! The Colonel advised the War Department that there is now no illegal traffic in narcotics in Japan. He said American forces have destroyed heroin valued at more than one million dollars.

KATE SMITH:

That, it seems to me, is great accomplishment. Fighting evil in this world is more important sometimes than fighting a battle, and it's good to know that poppy-growing in Japan as a major occupation has now been eliminated. When the American forces took over, there were 100,000 Korean farmers growing poppies for opium, and 300,000 Japanese poppy farms. Now there are none! That's one more victory to score up for our side!

(CLOSING COMMERCIAL)

Today, as you've heard me say on so many Fridays in the past, is Playhouse Day. It's the one day of the week when Jack Miller and the boys in our band, the various entertainers, engineer, sound man, electricians, page boys, and all the rest of our group get together for the rehearsals of our night show. Tonight marks our final broadcast of this season on that show, so it seems fitting for me now to say a little word about those who have worked with me all through the year. To you who listen, it's just another radio show closed for the summer, but to us who have been through many trials and triumphs together, who have shared problems and made last minute changes in script and rehearsed over and over again some brief spot which needed to be made right, the last show in June means good-byes and handshakes and good wishes as we go our separate ways for the summer. Some of our company will work in other shows; some will go to seashore or mountains or lakes for a well-earned vacation; and I think today all of us feel a bit sad thinking of the fun we've had together, of the laughs that have come up in our work, and of the minor tragedies avoided. I speak with mixed emotions, because I never like to say "good-bye," never like to think of a break in the dear and familiar routine, but I do want to express my thanks and appreciation today, which all too often is not spoken for those who work faithfully week after week, year after year, behind the scenes. And without those services, shows just would not go on. I want to say thanks, too, to all you folks who have listened each Friday evening. We'll be back on the job in October, trying to bring you a bigger and better weekly broadcast than we've ever given before.

As for these daytime talks, I'm very happy to say we'll be with you, Ted and I, as usual every day at high noon, straight through the summer. Late tonight, when the curtain goes down on the stage, I'll rush home and finish packing, and tomorrow morning bright and early, I'm driving to my summer home beside a lake up in the mountains. On Monday I'll be speaking to you from that spot I love so well. As for Ted, he gets around to so many places, I don't know...where will you be, Mr. C?

TED COLLINS:

Maybe Boston, maybe the mountains, maybe some place where the fish are biting! Anyway, Kathryn, wherever I find myself, I'll be right on the job as usual when high noon rolls around, and our broadcast will go on as always! That's a promise!

KATE SMITH:

Well, that's fine. And so, we'll all be together right through the summer. We'll bring you the news and stories and bits of philosophy we hope you like, being grateful for your friendship, your loyalty and your interest which makes these daily talks such a pleasure to us. So don't forget to tune in tonight for our final Friday night show of the season. Thanks for listenin' and good-bye, folks!

Posing with President Truman after Kate has given him the theme song for the Red Feather campaign.

KATE SMITH SPEAKS — WEDNESDAY, AUGUST 28TH, 1946

This broadcast is on the CD. Notice how cleverly Kate keeps Ted in line, as he has a hangover from the night before.

Hello, everybody! Ya know, there must be something in the air of pioneer lands that makes people energetic. Everybody in Alaska, for instance, has a side-line. Don Goodman, an executive of Alaska Airlines, is one example: after leaving his office, he may be seen in working clothes driving a bulldozer out to some construction project where he digs basements, levels roads, clears land, or what have you. Ben Edwards, traffic manager for the same airline company, builds houses on the side. Right now he's constructing ten homes to help ease the housing shortage in Anchorage.

TED COLLINS:

They're busy people, those Alaskans. A prominent banker, I understand, operates a beauty salon on the side. The manager of a night club has a junk yard. Those 20 hours of daylight during the summer months gives Alaskans time to engage in many activities besides their regular means of livelihood. Homesteading, trapping, fishing, prospecting and mining are all tempting occupations and Ralph Arnold, publisher of the Matanuska Valley Post, drives a bus on a night schedule from Anchorage to Palmer.

KATE SMITH:

It looks as though folks are getting things done up there in the land of the midnight sun. Now if the folks in this country would just follow their example, we might have some of that badly needed volume-production which we've all been waiting for in this postwar world!

(OPENING COMMERCIAL)

Well, science has been applying itself once again to the happiness of the American household, there has been a crop of new gadgets, and one of the best and simplest, I think, is a new table cover, made of a thin plastic that's so transparent you can hardly see it. You spread the cover over your table after you've put on your best linen cloth and all the food stains can be wiped off without ever coming in contact with the fine linen. This plastic cover, by the way, is very soft and so pliable it will drape over the corners of your table like a real cloth, and any housewife who's washed and ironed tablecloths hundreds of times in the course of the years will certainly appreciate the plastic cover.

TED COLLINS:

Science has also come forward recently with a gadget that appeals to me. No more need for stumbling in the dark and fumbling for that elusive light switch. A new lighted wall switch late has a pin-point glow lamp permanently sealed into its plastic case. When the light in the room is turned off, the light in the switch goes on automatically, and the other way around. The small light works only when every other bulb in the room has been extinguished.

KATE SMITH:

That's a fine idea, Ted. I suppose you'll have something like this installed in your summer home up here?

TED COLLINS:

I certainly will. That is, when I can get the materials to go ahead with the building. It's going to be quite a nice little place if all my plans on paper materialize.

KATE SMITH:

I'm sure it will. And despite all the headaches, it's a grand experience working on a place of your own. And now, Ted, what's new?

(NEWS)

(CLOSING COMMERCIAL)

"What's the use of wishing?" I heard a woman remark the other day. "Wishing won't make it so!" And my mind traveled back to another day and another woman, and a wish. It was a day in June, a warm sunny day when most folks were swimming, or riding around in their cars. But the woman I speak of was middle-aged. She was dressed in a faded housedress, partly covered by an equally faded gingham apron. Her sleeves were rolled above the elbow and arms and hands were plunged deep in a tub of soap-suds. Her face was flushed and shining, and she had a compelling light in her Irish blue eyes, as she made her wish. "I wish," she said impetuously "that I could get hold of a washing machine."

She needed one, there was no doubt about that, for her back yard blossomed with clothes lines full of the gay summer clothes of a dozen families. She was no struggling heroine of a romantic novel, no artist striving for recognition. She was, as she admitted frankly and without shame, a "wash woman." She had no talent for anything else, she told me, but she had a burning desire to own the little frame house which she rented a couple of years before. "And," she added emphatically, "I'm going to pay off a $700 mortgage this summer if the good Lord gives me strength. And I'm sure He will!"

It was about the middle of July when I stopped again to see her. Surrounded by all the clothes that belonged to others, she looked up and smiled. "How are you?" I asked, and she said heartily, "Oh, I'm just fine. I got my washing machine; it's a second-hand one, but it's good."

"What you need now is a mangler," I suggested. "Yes," she said, "I wish I had a mangler. I guess one will come along one of these days."

The other day I stopped again at the little white house with its strings of clean clothes fluttering on the lines in the morning sun. Once more I saw the washwoman, sleeves still rolled high, that beaming Irish smile still lighting her ruddy face. "Got my mangler," she announced triumphantly. "One of the people I wash for found an old one in their garage. It sure does save a lot of time."

"How about that mortgage?" I asked. "Need any help?"

"No" she answered proudly. "We want to take care of that ourselves. Both my boys are working in the grocery store, and we're doing fine!"

"What's the use of wishing...wishing won't make it so." That's what that other woman had said the other evening. I wonder if she knows exactly what a real wish is? A real wish, a yearning toward a dream, means more than the mouthing of a few words, more than idly glancing upward through darkness and murmuring a doggerel on a bright star. A real wish means struggle, and work, and elbow-grease; day in, day out, week in, week out. It means faith that what is needed will come to you, and means working without it until it arrives. It means toiling when others play. It means the kind of determination and concentration that will not recognize defeat.

Next time you think you want something badly, you might let your thoughts stray for a moment, to a washwoman in a little town who wished for a washing machine and a mangler and kept on working. A woman who, I'm sure, when the first of October comes along will have attained the summer goal she set for herself, and will be able to look proudly at the roof over her head and say: "This is my house. I earned it with my own two hands!" Think of her and make your earnest wish, and then go to work and make your wish come true.

Thanks for listenin' and good-bye, folks!

(BROADCAST #2543)

KATE SMITH SPEAKS —
MONDAY, DECEMBER 2ND, 1946

It's high noon in New York and time for Kate Smith, as our own Ted Collins usually announces, but I'll have to be my own announcer for a while, so I'll just say this is Kate Smith.

Ted is having problems with his heart and will be "on the bench" for several weeks. (He died of a heart attack at Lake Placid on May 27, 1964.)

No doubt many of you have wondered why Ted was missing from this program on Thanksgiving Day, on Friday, and again last evening on our Sunday broadcast. During our sixteen years of broadcasting, Ted has always been right here on the job with me, except when urgent out-of-town business prevented. Now, however, I'm very, very sorry to have to tell that it isn't business that's keeping him away from this microphone. It's because he isn't well. In fact, he hasn't been up to par for the last few weeks, but he kept on going. Now, his physician has ordered him to make a complete rest, and you folks who know Ted Collins through hearing his cheery voice every day at high noon will realize that it's a hard prescription for him to take! I know all of you join with me in hoping he'll be back with us soon, and I hope you'll add your fervent prayers to my own for his speedy and complete recovery to perfect health.

Meantime, I'm going to carry on as usual with the aid of various Columbia newscasters who will be glad to pinch-hit for Ted in bringing us the up-to-the-minute news each day. I'll never forget how Ted carried on in my stead for several weeks four years back when I was ill, and I only hope I'll be able to do as well now as he did then. Anyway, he's going to be listening in with a radio right beside his bed, so we better be good (laughing) or I'll sure hear from him!

(OPENING COMMERCIAL)

The veterans at the University of Buffalo have gone to war again...but this time, I think, it comes under the head of fun—though there IS an earnest crusade behind it. They're making war on the familiar blue jeans, plaid shirts, and droopy sweaters still affected by many American college girls. It looks, too, as if they've already won their battle! The leaders of the opposition, composed of Buffalo's 750 co-eds, are about to concede defeat. The girls admit that the old collegiate clothes are fast going out the window in favor of dressier styles, with high heels and stockings coming back after a long exile. Yes, glamour is back! That's good news to all vets; they don't like carelessly dressed girls. They say they didn't come home from foxholes and battle stations to go out with a lot of "chicks" dressed like sad sacks! (Laughing) Nevertheless, they do sometimes, whether they like it or not. I guess it all depends on how much they care for that certain girl. Anyway, the boys better think carefully about one important phase of this glamour business. If they make the girls dress up in frills and furbelows now, those girls will expect to have plenty of pretty things after they get married! Judging from present prices on feminine wearing apparel, those boys are going to get quite a shock, after they've said "I do"! Just wait (laughing) until those clothes bills for the little woman start coming in, boys!

And now, we're going to switch you over to Mr. Harry Marble, who will pinch hit for Ted and bring us the news of the world.

(NEWS)

Thank you Mr. Marble, for Ted and myself,

In the same news behind the news, I hear that the Emerald Isle is now the number-one land of plenty! Tourists to Ireland for this year of 1946 will number about a million people, and what they find in Ireland is plenty of good food and lots of it: filet mignons, ice-cream sundaes, cream as rich as the Irish brogue, and stores crammed with merchandise!

I'm mentioning the Emerald Isle right now because I got talking with a taxi driver last evening on the way home from the Playhouse after our show and he said he'd just gotten back from a visit to his folks in Ireland. He insisted that it's Paradise there these days, compared with the rest of the world: a land of milk and honey, magnificent scenery, hotels and cafes freshly painted and decorated and very gay—AND not too expensive. He said a fine dinner, grandly served by waiters in swallow-tail coats, costs about $1.50 in American money. The juke boxes are going full blast there, too, he says, and incidentally, they cost only a penny a record! Ireland listeners are thinking of taking a trip to Eire, I'd better add that outgoing baggage is carefully checked, and visitors are permitted to take only a limited number of articles out of the country.

(CLOSING COMMERCIAL)

Our city streets are dark these December evenings, but strikes notwithstanding, the lights on children's indoor Christmas trees will glow this Christmas as they always have, and I'm certainly glad to report that news! Santa Claus will still be able to see his way around and leave those toys for good little girls and boys. Mr. John D. Small, Civilian Production Administrator, has ruled that the 21-state dim-out, banning ornamental lighting because of the coal strike, was not meant to cover indoor Christmas trees in homes. The ruling does apply, however, to trees in stores and other business buildings—and all outdoor Christmas trees.

According to a survey made here the other day, trees will cost about the same as last year, though the coal strike may even change that. Most dealers are optimistic, though. It's predicted that a balsam six-feet high will cost from $2.50 to $3.00. A six-foot tree is a huge one; trees need not be quite so large for most of us, and they'll be less expensive. A little one is pretty and takes less time and money to decorate. Speaking of those sparkling decorations reminds me of the legend of the century. An Arabian wayfarer, 'tis said, brought to the western world of Europe the tale that on the night of the Lord's nativity, all the trees for miles around burst forth with brightly-colored ripened fruits and beautiful flowers. His story spread up and down the land until it became a widespread belief that the miracle of the fruits and flowers had come to pass in memory of the birth of Christ.

And so, gradually, according to the lovely legend, people began to set up little trees and decorate them with flowers and fruits and ornaments made by their own hands. This thousand-year-old legend has given us one of our most inspiring Christmas customs. Among my earliest memories is the recollection of the glittering tinsel star at the top of our Christmas tree. I still have that tinsel star. It's a little bit tarnished now, a little bit wobbly, but on each blessed Christmas Eve it gets its place of honor above all the other ornaments, and to me it grows lovelier and more steadfast with each passing year!

And now, it's time for me to be on my way, but I'll be with you all again tomorrow at this time. Thanks for listenin' and goodbye, folks!

KATE SMITH SPEAKS —
MONDAY, FEBRUARY 24TH, 1947

Hello, everybody! I hope you all had a nice weekend. I had company over Saturday and Sunday, and we talked about everything from the United Nations' new site here in New York City to gardening and how to bake a perfect cake!

TED COLLINS:
And did you bake that perfect cake, Kathryn?

KATE SMITH:
(Laughing) Oh, I don't know how perfect it was but it vanished quickly...and you know what they always say about the "proof of the pudding!" As for the gardening, my African violets are blooming their heads off. And, as for the United Nations site, all visitors to New York are interested in seeing the spot along the East River where the six-block world capital is going to be.

TED COLLINS:
The program is being considerably enlarged, Kathryn, to improve the land surrounding the site. When the first re-zoning program was disclosed, civic groups and United Nations officials protested that the city's plan were too limited. The commission has now extended the improvement area to include several extra blocks. It's going to be quite a place when it's completed.

KATE SMITH:
With as important a group from all corners of the world coming into our midst, we must make sure that the spot is one which not only New Yorkers, but all Americans can point to with pride.

TED COLLINS:
What else did you do over the weekend, Kathryn?

KATE SMITH:
Well, for one thing I had two radio shows to do yesterday, T.C. I took a look at the sportsman's show which you saw last week when it first opened, Ted.

TED COLLINS:
How did you like it?

KATE SMITH:
I thought it was wonderful, Ted. What always fascinates me most at those shows are the exhibits of log-cabins and camping equipment: portable stoves, camp cookery, and all those things. I was also interested in some equipment for the lazy fisherman.

TED COLLINS:
Fishermen are not lazy!

KATE SMITH:
Don't try to tell ME that, Ted! (Laughing) Often on my walks along the mountain trail I've come across fishermen sitting on the bank of a lake half asleep, paying almost no attention to their fishing rods or lines.

TED COLLINS:
They were probably taking a rest while the fish weren't biting, maybe in the middle of the day. But what about this fishing gear you mentioned?

KATE SMITH:
Oh, it's some sort of a rig called "Kompanion." It hasn't any wheels, but it gives you a chair to sit in, a rod rest, a cutting board for bait, and a tackle box. It can be folded up and carried under one arm.

TED COLLINS:
Sounds all right, but I'll stick to my old guide boat.

KATE SMITH:
Well, this equipment I saw is supposed to be for men who fish in the ocean, surf-casting or fishing from the end of a pier.

TED COLLINS:
You know, it's a funny thing about fishermen. I think they go through various phases. As small boys, they probably catch sunfish and catfish in a small pond. Later, when they grow up, if they have the opportunity, they go for the big ones: sail-fish, tuna and such. Then, after they've caught their sail-fish and their monster tuna, they're very likely to go on to fly fishing for smaller game fish. After I caught my big sail-fish off the Florida coast and got some tuna off Nova Scotia, I was quite content to go back to the mountain streams for trout, and the mountain lakes for bass. But then, it's all fine sport, fishing!

(OPENING COMMERCIAL)

Well, to law-abiding citizens it certainly was disturbing news when word came from Havana, Cuba, that Lucky Luciano, a notorious and distinctly unsavory racketeer, was doing business in that island republic. This man, who for years was known as the "Vice King of Broadway," a dealer in the most loathsome types of crime, had somehow made his way to Cuba.

He was prosecuted for his crimes in 1936 by Governor Dewey, who was then District Attorney, and was sentenced to serve between thirty and fifty years in prison. Later he was released from prison and deported to Italy.

Lucky Luciano, described by Governor Dewey as the most dangerous and important criminal in the country, now lives in luxury in Havana.

His business? Reports say that he is masterminding gambling

activities in the two places in that city where gambling is permitted by law. There, at the Jockey Club and the National Casino, this evil, dangerous man rubs elbows each night, with some of America's most famous celebrities.

But how did he get there? Who is responsible for the issuance of a visa to this foul enemy of society, this dealer in white slavery?

Reports say that he has friends down there, influential friends; friends who are willing to swap protection for an inside, expert knowledge of the underworld and how to make money outside the fringe of the law.

No one knows whether Lucky Luciano's visa is for temporary or permanent resident, or if he is just there on a visit. Then he must have signed a pledge not to work while there, but sometimes such things can be overlooked if one has political connections.

The people of New York don't need to be told what that would mean, but perhaps the people of Cuba do.

Lucky Luciano, they say, is publicity-shy and subdued now, and with good reason, for he knows that the white glare of the spotlight might send him right back where he was sent before: clear out of this hemisphere, or if it's legally possible, back to prison for a good long time.

CBS didn't like this editorial and it was a big factor in Kate's leaving them in June.

(CLOSING COMMERCIAL)

KATE SMITH:
The idea men who specialize in easier living have opened up their sample kits again. And this time they're displaying everything from ready-built houses to gadgets for discouraging the old trick of sweeping dirt under the rug.

The display marks the opening in Chicago today of the National Association of Home Builders Convention, and for the next four days more than six thousand homebuilders, all looking ahead to their biggest year, will wrestle with the problem of how to get along with price controls and the labor shortage, both of which, they say, are retarding home construction.

And just to add a little window-dressing to the gathering, manufacturers are exhibiting a collection of postwar devices that's enough to bring a gleam to the eye of every house and gadget-hungry American.

TED COLLINS:
One of the big steel corporations, for example, is showing an arch-ribbed, Quonset-type house designed to sell complete for four thousand dollars. And home-builders say they'll finance it for a mere thirty-five dollars a month.

Or, if you already have a house but are addicted to bumping into protruding doors, the gadgeteers have solved your problem with a door which folds into the woodwork like an accordion.

KATE SMITH:
And if you are one of those folks who just can't help stumbling over the furniture between the light button and your bed, there's a delayed-action switch which allows you up to three minutes to make the trip.

The "dust-under-the-rug" habit is cured by the installation of convenient dust chutes that are guaranteed to whisk away that little pile of dust in a twinkling.

For one hundred and sixty-five dollars you can purchase a radio-controlled apparatus that opens your garage door as soon as you touch a button on your automobile dashboard.

TED COLLINS:
The compact utility units are back, too. You will soon be able to

purchase a deluxe model which includes kitchen, bath, heat equipment, and laundry, all sold in one neat package.

KATE SMITH:
But, before you rush out to buy any of these fine items, perhaps you'd better wait until the Homebuilders Association finds the answer to the housing shortage. And at their Convention in Chicago this week they are honestly trying to do just that.

Thanks for listenin' and goodbye, folks!

KATE SMITH SPEAKS —
WEDNESDAY, JUNE 4TH, 1947

Hello, everybody!

Sometime this week I hope to visit an interesting display sponsored by the American Hobby Federation here in New York City. It's the Ninth Annual American Doll Show that opened yesterday in one of the large department stores.

There are thousands and thousands of rare and unusual dolls on display, anywhere from centuries to a few weeks old. Some of them actually represent the 16th century. Some are as small as a mere fraction of an inch, while others are several feet high.

Among the exhibits is the tiniest doll portrait ever made of George Washington. There are native leather Moroccan dolls and medicine men, with doctors and nurse dolls, just to name a few.

But one of the exhibits I'm most interested in seeing is a large and colorful collection representing many biblical characters. There are David and Goliath, King Solomon, and Joseph in his coat of many colors in this set of dolls. The dolls in this collection are being shown by the woman who made them, Mrs. Max Forman of Philadelphia, Pa.

So if you like dolls, big ones or small ones, antique or modern, dolls from every corner of the earth, they can be seen any day this week in New York and it's an event I don't want to miss.

(OPENING COMMERCIAL)

KATE SMITH:

Out in Chicago, there's a man pleading for a return to the good old-fashioned way of raising babies. This man, one Hugh Randall, wants mothers to go back to their rocking chair and the "Little Baby Bunting" song routine.

Mr. Randall doesn't pretend to be an expert raising children, but he does know music and the effect it has on everyone, regardless of age. And today he sounded off on his theories at a convention of the National Association of Music Merchants of which he is a member.

And you know, I think he has something there. Give the baby a sense of music appreciation from the very day he is born. He may not grown up to be great musician, but he will have gained a faithful friend. For music is just that, an understanding friend in time of trouble, a gay friend in your happy hours.

Like Mr. Randall, I began life when the cradle and "Rock-a-bye-bye" were companions in every household, and I like to think that those were truly the good old days. Unfortunately, I did not take my mother's advice and study music. Even to this very day, I can't read a note, and many times I have regretted my indifference to her advice. But in our modern times, all too often youngsters are given no musical background until they're old enough to play a musical instrument. And as Mr. Randall says, by then, youngsters will not show much interest in practicing music. And that's too bad, because I'm sure all of them would find life's path much easier as they grow older if they knew how to enjoy to the fullest the wonderful music of all nations. Music is indeed a force that helps bind the world together.

And now, Ted, what's new?

(NEWS)

KATE SMITH:

And in the news behind the news, it's graduation day today for the girls of Radcliffe College, in Cambridge, Massachusetts. It's a long time since I've been in Cambridge, but I can see this lovely spot in my mind's eye and the historic college buildings of Radcliffe and Harvard, and my best wishes go out to all the girl graduates on this day which is so important to them.

While we're on the subject of young women, Ted, have you seen the June issue of the magazine "Seventeen?"

TED COLLINS:
No Kathryn, I haven't. I do read quite a lot but I've never gotten around to getting interested in a teen-agers' magazine.

KATE SMITH:
Then, may I suggest that you do. I think it would be smart for all adults to examine this June issue, which is called "It's All Yours." You see, for this one month the magazine has been completely taken over by girls and boys of seventeen or under. They contribute the articles, the short stories, the fashion notes, the motion picture and book reviews, the art work and all the rest, and what they have to say, I think, is important reading in these times when almost everybody is criticizing youth. Ted Thompson has a fine article about drinking...and whether 17-year-old...a girl from the Bronx, in New York City, named Lenora Helman, has an excellent piece called "It's Right To Be Wrong" meaning, of course, it's the right thing to admit you're wrong when you are, and to say you're sorry. This June issue of "Seventeen" is a good, sound presentation of what our teen-agers are thinking, and I recommend it for June reading for young AND old!

And while I'm on the subject of children, out in Chicago today, a speaker at the fiftieth Annual Convention of the National Congress of Parents and Teachers declared that 350,000 of our teachers have given up their jobs in recent years, mainly because of low salaries and embarrassing social restrictions.

This is a deplorable situation. I fear we are forgetting that the school children of today are the active citizens of tomorrow. We want them to grow up to be fine, upright men and women. And they will, I am sure, if we have teachers who are also fine, upright men and women.

But we can have them only if we pay them salaries commensurate with their training and ability, and if we accept them in our community life as the competent, interesting, and cooperative persons they are. What do you think?

(CLOSING COMMERCIAL)

If you are planning a summer vacation that will take you into middle Tennessee, there's one spot you won't want to miss. It's a stately old mansion located on Highway 70 South, just outside the town of McMinnville, in Warren County. It is a handsome place, shaded by graceful trees, and set back on a roomy, velvet-green lawn. If you go riding by, glancing casually, you'll probably think it's someone's fine old country estate, but appearances are misleading sometimes. They most certainly are in this case.

You see, this fine old mansion is the new Warren County poor farm, better known as the Magness Home for the Aged, and it's a model institution that could be copied to good advantage by many other counties throughout these United States. It's operated on the theory that homes for the aged and poor need not be the heartless institutions they all too often turn out to be. At the Magness House the residents spend their sunset-days in a friendly, comfortable, and truly home-like atmosphere. The superintendent is a quiet spoken middle-aged former mechanic. He and his wife direct the operation of the farm. Altogether there are 14 guests ranging in age from 60 to 95. Of the 14, half are both able and eager to help out about the place. These four women and three men aid with the laundering and mending, they wash dishes, set up tables, wait on the invalids, feed the livestock, and help in the fields. No one is forced to work, but bear in mind, they love to keep busy. Right here, I'd like to interrupt my story by stressing this fact. In all too many homes for the aged and infirm, the old folks are regarded simply as burdens. No one ever stops to think, apparently, how overjoyed they would be to have some little useful task to perform, something to add variety to their monotonous lives and help to make the time pass quickly and profitably.

This splendid example of county care for the aged and poor was made possible by a wealthy McMinnville philanthropist, the late Mr. William Magness. In his will, he left $50,000 for the establishment and maintenance of the home in honor of his mother, and the institution certainly reflects great credit on the farsighted Mr. Magness, as well as other residents of Warren County, Tennessee, whose tax money helps support the home.

I speak of this especially today because I've been hearing a lot lately of the ghastly conditions in many private and public institutions around the country in the care of their poor and aged. What about the one in your county, or your city or town? How is it being conducted? What is being done with YOUR tax money which supports it? Old people need something more than barely enough to keep body and soul together; they need comfort and happiness and entertainment and activity. And surely, in the twilight of a long life, they deserve it!

Thanks for listenin' and good-bye, folks!

KATE SMITH SPEAKS —
FRIDAY, JUNE 20TH, 1947

Kate says goodbye to CBS, but where's Ted? She will return to CBS-TV in 1960 for a 20-week series.

It's high noon in New York, and this is Kate Smith saying hello, everybody! Our Mr. Ted Collins is among the missing this morning, so we'll go along without him the best way we can. And the first thing I want to mention is the state of West Virginia. Somehow or other, I don't think we mention West Virginia very often and I'm sorry about that, for we have many listeners and good friends there. Anyway, I'm sending a very special greeting to that Southern state now, in honor of its birthday. It was exactly 84 years ago on this date that West Virginia entered the union as a full-fledged state. I understand it's a legal holiday down there today, and I can just imagine how gay it is, with flags flying and other special commemorations of the anniversary.

And now to take a little look at another state we don't mention very often, the New England state of Connecticut. The parishioners of a church up in Westport, Connecticut, are literally trading the past for the future this week. They're selling some six hundred of their family heirlooms at auction, so that their children may have a youth center and a new church building.

The parishioners of the Christ and Holy Trinity Church decided that many of the treasured antiques tucked away in their attic were of no use to anyone that way. On the other hand, their children needed a center where they could gather for entertainment as well as spiritual training. So, they reasoned, why not sell some of the heirlooms to help raise money for a really useful project?

The objects they're offering include two fine pre-Revolutionary period spinning wheels, some lovely antique chairs and china, a colonial sideboard and kerosene lamps. The people who are giving up these family treasures are making the sacrifices gladly. They know that the money will be used to give their children, and their neighbors' children, a safe place to spend their leisure hours. And in doing this, the parishioners of this Westport, Connecticut church are building a better community for the future. It sounds like a highly praise-worthy project and oh, how I wish I could get up there tomorrow to take a look around. I'm an incurable collector of old things. Ted Collins laughs and calls them junk, and lots of other people can't understand how we antiquers enjoy picking up all sorts of odds and ends reminiscent of an earlier day, but honestly, to me there's a real thrill in every beautiful piece of old china, every bit of early American glass. I even get excited about old things I'm not really collecting, for I cannot look at any heirloom without thinking of the associations of its past, without dreaming a little and wondering who, in years gone by, treasured it as part of the home, but I guess I better forget about collecting antiques for the moment and talk a little bit now about the present and those handy Muffinaires, made of good modern aluminum.

(OPENING COMMERCIAL)

Every now and then, for the past several months, I've talked about the high prices of food and clothing, and food prices, some of them, still are way out of line, it seems to me. But in all fairness, I must say that in our big department stores, and most of the specialty shops around this big city, prices are definitely more reasonable on many items. Dresses and hats (pretty ones, too) can be had for a very modest sum indeed. Curtains are a little lower in price than they were three or four months ago, and while furniture is an expensive item for new homes, on the bright side of the ledger, kitchen equipment, china, and other necessities carry lower price tags than they have in a long, long time.

And for you folks who are planning a trip to New York and are still hearing about the crowds and the difficulties in getting theatre tickets, let me say, if you're coming to New York City, for instance, I had lunch in a tearoom in the vicinity of Times Square (which is usually packed at 1 p.m.) and instead of a long, impatient line waiting to be served, I found there wasn't any line at all. I was shown a vacant table right away, and my lunch was served efficiently. And one of our hit plays is running and I was able to buy two excellent seats at box office prices for a performance three evenings later. I couldn't help smiling to myself as I recalled what a different situation existed on a few months ago. Later, I went to the housewares department of a big store in midtown to buy a food-chopper. There were only a few customers and several clerks eager to wait upon them. I got what I wanted without delay, and I thought to myself, as I had at the theatre, quite a difference between now and those war and early post-war days. No crowds, no clerks unwilling to serve people, and no chasing around to one place after another to buy a couple of theatre tickets...and no standing on long lines for lunch!

And now, let's see, I guess there's no time like the present to remind all of you that we'll be on the air with songs and festivities this coming Sunday as usual. If you look for us on your dial when it's 6:30 p.m. New York Daylight Time, you'll find us right there, ready and willing to entertain you: Jack Miller and the boys in the band, the Four Chicks and Chuck, and yours truly. We'll have the music and songs you love to hear, and I hope all my radio friends will make a note to be with us on Sunday.

Speaking of singing reminds me of dancing, and dancing reminds me that the Saturday afternoon summer square dances will start tomorrow here in our town on the mall in our Central Park and they'll be held every Saturday afternoon right through September 20th. You know, this free dancing on the green is a joy, whether you trip the light fantastic, or just look on. Watching folk dances, especially out in the open under the green trees, and listening to the gay, spirited music, is a very pleasant summer pastime, indeed.

(CLOSING COMMERCIAL)

And now in the little time we have left, I want to say salute-and-farewell to an association that Ted Collins and I have enjoyed for almost seventeen years! That's a long, long time, seventeen years, but I look back on every one of those years with pleasure, and feel a pang of keen regret at their passing. But, I look forward also to the future, knowing that all things change, and that often, changes are good. And a jingle I recall from childhood passes gently through my mind, "Hours fly, flowers die, new men, new ways, pass by..."

Today, Ted and I are saying goodbye, not to radio which I guess will always claim us, but to this network. We will be on the air every day when it's high noon in New York as usual, and you can find us on another spot of your dial. I have learned much during all these 17 years, have had many rich and wonderful experiences, enjoyed the friendships and the contacts with all those who have been a part of Columbia. And as we leave these pleasant associations, I want to express my thanks and my appreciation for many kindnesses from Mr. William S. Paley, friend through all the Columbia years, right straight down the line through engineers, soundmen, secretaries, typists, telephone operators, and all the many other employees of the company. I have received help and cooperation and encouragement in my work, and I am grateful. My mind goes back over so many great occasions we have shared together; the times during the war when we all worked together 24 hours at a stretch, selling millions of dollars worth of War Bonds, times like Pearl Harbor and the tragic death of the late President Roosevelt, and ever so many other occasions when, at a moment's notice, we all had to change out plans, scrap our ideas, and work feverishly day and night to meet some new situation. I remember, too, how the Columbia folks put all their vast facilities at our disposal on that evening years ago, when I was called to the White House to sing for the King and Queen of England. We had a Kate Smith Hour that evening that was to be put in our Playhouse here in New York City. The show had to go on, but also I had to sing my songs for our royal visitors. And so, everybody pitched in with a will, and arranged what then seemed to all of us a marvelous feat of engineering. My show went on in

New York, with its audience. My orchestra performed on the Playhouse stage, and as they played my accompaniment here, I, in Washington, through the miracle of radio, was enabled to sing along with them, and do my part of our regular show, being on hand at the White House, and a few minutes later, singing for President and Mrs. Roosevelt and their distinguished guests. But I mustn't reminisce too long, there are still other acknowledgments to be made, other thank-yous to be said.

For, as we say farewell to Columbia, we say farewell to the General Foods Corporation, our sponsor for almost twelve years, and I feel a little bit sad. Among our associates at General Foods, I want to mention especially Mr. Clarence Francis, Mr. Charlie Mortimer, Mrs. Bobby Myers, and Mr. Clarence Eldridge. Mr. Eldridge was the man who originally gave us the opportunity of going on radio for General Foods. These men I have mentioned, and also Mrs. Meyers, are great leaders in American business. They have fine ideals: they stand for what is good in business. Their products are fine, and I have always been proud to recommend them. You who listen, know that...you do not honestly believe in...I have always felt that General Foods and its products...and I have enjoyed my association with the Company...So, it is only fitting in this last moment of farewell to these sponsors, that I express my thoughts, tender my thanks, and wish them Godspeed for the future.

Ted Collins wasn't able to be here with me on the program today, so I'd like to add that the thanks and the appreciation to Columbia and General Foods are said on his behalf as well as my own.

Yes, it's the end of a happy cycle today, and the beginning of a new cycle because, don't forget, we'll be with you as usual next Monday, when it's high noon in New York, only we'll be on another network. Be sure to join us. Look for us on your dial! Meantime, have a very happy weekend!

Thanks for listenin' and good-bye, folks!

III: The Postwar Era

Kate switched to the Mutual Broadcasting System in June, 1947.

KATE SMITH SPEAKS — MONDAY, JUNE 23, 1947

Today it's "Hello, Mutual," on WOR, from which "Kate Smith Speaks" will broadcast for the next four years.

Hello, everybody! I hope you all had a very pleasant weekend, doing the things you wanted most to do, and finding time to get out into the fresh air and sunshine. As for me, I had a lovely, busy weekend, and this morning my heart is light in the thought that, along with many old friends who have been joining us at high noon for these many years, nine to be exact, we are welcoming today a large number of new friends in cities and towns across the nation, for this program marks our first regular daytime broadcast on this network. For our old friends, I'd like to say this: though we are heard now at a new place on the dial, we're just the same people as always, and we'll talk generally on a large variety of subjects just as we have in the past. We're still your neighbors; we've just moved that's all, to a house a little way down the block. For our new listeners, I want to say welcome; we hope you'll be sure to join us every day, Monday through Friday when it's high noon in New York, when we'll discuss all sorts of subjects interesting to the so-called "little people" of this old U.S.A. (who incidentally, are the big people, for they are the backbone of America.) And each day Ted will discuss the latest world news. I may express an opinion because I do feel strongly on certain subjects. But it must be understood that those opinions represent my own thoughts and ideas. If you don't agree with me, I won't mind a bit. And, I might add, whenever you feel in the mood to write to us, we'll be grateful for your letters and for your interest. Just address your letters to me in New York City, and not to the station which you are listening.

And now, a message from our sponsor!

(OPENING COMMERCIAL)

KATE SMITH:

If you're planning to spend you summer vacation this year seeing America, just any part of it, you'll be glad to hear that the welcome mat is out on practically everyone's doorstep.

Twenty-three million persons are expected to visit the National Parks this year.

Just one word of warning for those of you who are headed for the larger parks, such as Yosemite, Yellowstone, or Glacier: be sure to make your hotel reservations right away, for those larger parks will be especially popular.

TED COLLINS:

If you're wondering how easy you'll find transportation, listen to what the American Automobile Association and several other agencies have to say. They expect sixty-million persons to take their vacation this year in twenty-million cars. The Association of American Railroads says vacationers will find more accommodations available because of the easing-up of military traffic.

KATE SMITH:

And the Air Transport Association reveals that summer airlines reservations, both domestic and foreign, are well ahead of last year.

So if you haven't completed your plans yet and do want to travel, either at home or abroad, better make those reservations now. And wherever you go, whatever you do, I hope you have the best vacation ever.

And now Ted, what's new?

(NEWS)

And in the news behind the news, I'd like to toss a few verbal roses now in the direction of Salt Lake City, Utah, and the school children there who make up the school safety patrol! Out in Salt Lake City, parents don't worry any more about bad traffic accidents when they send their youngsters off to learn their three "Rs," because the school safety patrol has the wonderful record of no serious accidents on streets adjacent to schools for the past 18 years! Since 1929, there have been no fatalities and no major accidents among the boys and girls using the crosswalks supervised by the safety patrol. The members of the patrol are all school children, trained by regular police officers. They give up their own leisure time to learn and practice safety rules that will save the lives of their friends and classmates. The more than 700 junior officers whose school year is just ending looked after some 32,000 school children. They did a mighty fine job, too, with a 100 percent safety record. And best of all, all the youngsters in Salt Lake City are learning what some of us grown-ups sometimes forget; that courtesy, when practiced by both pedestrians and motorists, will eliminate 75 percent of all accidents. Just think of that! What a simple way, by kindness and consideration, to LET THE LIVING, LIVE!

AND NOW, YOUR LOCAL ANNOUNCER...

(CLOSING COMMERCIAL)

KATE SMITH:
You know, Ted, the whole nation is buzzing with talk about our possible Presidential candidates in 1948, but we haven't heard very much about the wives of those men, and one of whom might be elected as the head of our Government.

TED COLLINS:
And you think maybe we should consider the ladies a bit?

KATE SMITH:
Yes, I most certainly do. The seven wives of America's possible candidates are very different in temperament, and although no

man will be nominated because of his wife, it's interesting, I think, to know what the First Lady would be like in each case. Pat Lockridge, of the Woman's Home Companion staff, went around the country interviewing them and she's come up with the neat little thumbnail sketches of each. Mrs. Truman, already in the White House, has settled nicely into her job as First Lady and wouldn't mind staying there.

Bess Truman will remain in the White House until January 1953. Rumor has it, however, that she was not all that thrilled to be First Lady.

TED COLLINS:
(Lightly) And Mrs. Dewey, no doubt, wouldn't mind moving in!

KATE SMITH:
That's where you're wrong! Mrs. Thomas E. Dewey is one of the most retiring of the seven wives. She's pretty, petite, and always smartly dressed, but she likes privacy, can't make a speech, and is frank to admit she wishes her husband were just practicing law, so her family could lead a normal, private life.

TED COLLINS:
Mrs. Robert A. Taft, I hear, is an excellent speaker, campaigns for her husband all the time, and makes pretty good speeches, for a woman!

KATE SMITH:
What do you mean, "for a woman?" You'd better withdraw those words, Mr. Collins!

TED COLLINS:
I'll take that suggestion under advisement! What about Mrs. Arthur Vandenberg?

KATE SMITH:
Oh, after 20 years in Washington, Mrs. Vandenberg has taken over the social duties that would fall to the Vice President's lady,

if we had a Vice President. She takes care of all her husband's personal correspondence, makes appointments for him, and is his super-confidential secretary. She even buys his suits! But she has no keen desire to be mistress of the White House. Incidentally, Mrs. Vandenberg, tall, handsome and in her early sixties, is an especially good cook. As for Mrs. Harold Stassen, she's very quiet, and when she was asked if she'd like to live in the White House, Esther Stassen said: "I don't think it necessary for any woman to worry about that until she gets there!" Mrs. John Bricker answered that same question this way: "There's nothing I'd like more!" As for Mrs. Earl Warren, wife of the Governor of California, she'll stay in the background no matter what happens. She's never made a speech. The Governor explained that once. He said, "We have one rule in our house! I do the talking in public and my wife does the talking at home!"

TED COLLINS:
Well, these seven ladies sound like a fine group! I'm glad we don't have to vote for the wives, come election. If we did, I'd probably break the law and sneak out and vote for all seven of 'em!

KATE SMITH:
My, you're in a gentle mood this morning!

Thanks for listenin' and good-bye, folks!

Collins had all the "Kate Smith Speaks" scripts saved in Morocco-bound volumes, hers in green and his news segments in burgundy.

KATE SMITH SPEAKS — MONDAY, AUGUST 11TH, 1947

Hello, everybody! I hope you all had a very nice weekend, a good rest and the chance that the weekend always brings to store up a little extra energy, find a little extra pleasure, and follow your own special inclination of reading, or getting out into the country, or spending a few hours at your favorite hobby, whatever it happens to be. My favorite summer hobby is gardening. Gardening accomplishes so many things: it gives you a chance to get into the sun and fresh air, exercises those back and shoulder muscles, and if you have that green thumb that most gardeners insist they possess, it makes the flowers and vegetables grow and flourish! As for you, Ted, we all know what YOUR favorite pastime is, and I'll bet I know where YOU'D like to be for the next three days!

TED COLLINS:
Where?

KATE SMITH:
Down on the southern coast of Alabama!

TED COLLINS:
That's the spot, Kathryn, because today, tomorrow and Wednesday are the dates for one of America's greatest fishing celebrations—the Alabama Deep-Sea Fishing Rodeo.

KATE SMITH:
What on earth is a fishing Rodeo? Do the fisherman go round with a rope, bulldogging the poor fish, or do they do their casting from the saddle?

TED COLLINS:
My, but you're full of original ideas this Monday morning! According to Mr. Webster and his best-seller, the good old dictionary, a rodeo is a round-up, and a round-up is a gathering-in of scattered persons or things. Fishermen are undoubtedly scattered persons - scattered all over the country. This fishing rodeo is the fifteenth annual celebration. Of course, there was none during the war years. Actually the meet is a king-sized fishing contest for king-sized fish. The contestants are judged on points; a tarpon, sailfish, or ling counts 500. A shark is 100 but it must weigh more than 50 pounds.

KATE SMITH:
Don't they count any nice little fish?

TED COLLINS:
Well, yes, but not much. The lowest number of points is ten, for Spanish mackerel and speckled trout.

KATE SMITH:
They make very tasty eating. I think maybe you ought to get more points for them—after all, nobody wants to eat a shark!

TED COLLINS:
Now isn't that just like a woman! Just because you like the taste! It's the fish that are hardest to catch that rate the count and the prizes, incidentally, are magnificent. The grand prize is a speed-boat, and there are outboard motors and many other awards.

KATE SMITH:
Will they have a fish-fry?

TED COLLINS:
Yes, tomorrow night they're having what's advertised as the world's largest fish-fry.

KATE SMITH:
Now, that's something I'd like to be in on. However, though we

may not have the world's largest up here in the mountains, we can have our own little fish fry—fresh fish out of the lake, cooked right beside the lake!

AND NOW, A MESSAGE FROM OUR SPONSOR!

(OPENING COMMERCIAL)

One of the items I'm glad to see returning to our midst is the old tried-and-true tea-wagon, the little cart of the early 1900s complete with its glass topped tray, its lower shelf and its baby-carriage handle to be pushed about on rubber-tired wheels and save the steps of the busy home-maker. I bought an old tea-wagon at a country auction last summer. It wasn't old enough to be called an "antique," yet it had a certain charm I couldn't resist.

TED COLLINS:
You probably couldn't resist the price, Kathryn. Women always go for bargains, whether they need 'em or not!

KATE SMITH:
Well, that may have been true at the time. I paid $4 for it, as I remember, and when I piled it into the station wagon and carried it back here, I didn't know that in the days to come it would be a very useful piece of furniture. Now, I see by the ads, they're making tea-wagons—modern ones.

TED COLLINS:
What do you use a tea-wagon for?

KATE SMITH:
(Laughing) Why, tea, of course! And plates of little cakes and sandwiches are put on the lower shelf. I even use mine for magazines and books, to be wheeled about in the garden or on the porch. And in winter, when plants are brought in from the garden, it makes a very decorative plant stand which can be moved with ease from window to window to catch the sun. It's also an extra right-hand for clearing the dining room table

quickly. A tea-wagon has any number of uses and I'm glad they're coming back into circulation. And now, Ted, what's new?

(NEWS)

KATE SMITH:
And in the news behind the news, when William Odom completed his round-the-world flight, he had accomplished more than a new record. He had fulfilled a boyhood dream, and he paid tribute to his hero and to one of America's favorite comedians, Will Rogers.

TED COLLINS:
Well, Kate, he had planned to drop a wreath on the Alaskan spot where Mr. Post and Mr. Rogers met their deaths on a flight back in 1935. He carried the wreath, which contained a scrap of fabric from the Post plane, nearly all the way round the world. But when he landed at Anchorage, Alaska, the Commandant of Ellmendorf Field asked that the wreath instead be mounted on a plaque and hung in the Officers Club.

So, Bill Odom left the wreath at the Officers' Club, and took off again.

KATE SMITH:
When he landed at Chicago, he had kept a 14-year-old promise to Wiley Post, who made the first solo round-the-world flight in 1933. Bill Odom had flown around the world alone, but he feels that his flight is not comparable to Wiley Post's, who did it the hard way, in the days when navigating was done entirely on a pencil and paper basis. However, both William Odom and Wiley Post set records of which America can well be proud.

I'll be back in a few moments but first, OUR ANNOUNCER:

(CLOSING COMMERCIAL)

KATE SMITH:

For those of you who love the old songs, the lovely songs that never die, here's a story, a story of how one of those songs came into being. In a hotel room in Riverside, California, many years ago, a woman paused as she was dressing for dinner, just as many of us pause, to watch from the window the fading of day into night. She had had a pleasant day with friends she loved, and now, as she stood watching the twilight shadows wrapping the earth in a soft gray shawl, she said with a sigh of pure happiness, "It has truly been a perfect day."

Suddenly, acting on impulse, she stepped to a table and began to write. The words began to take shape under her sure fingers, and those words she wrote have become familiar to all of us:

> "WHEN YOU COME TO THE END OF A PERFECT DAY,
> AND YOU SIT ALONE WITH YOUR THOUGHTS,
> WHILE THE CHIMES RING OUT WITH A CAROL GAY,
> FOR THE JOY THAT THE DAY HAS BROUGHT..."

In the intervals of dressing, hurrying from dresser to table and back again, she set down two stanzas. Then she tucked the slip of paper away and forgot it. But the words remained in her subconscious memory and months later, on another midsummer night, they rose spontaneously to her lips. She was driving with some friends, when she began to sing softly the words she had written that evening in Riverside. The melody came naturally, without thought or effort. "You've composed a new song, haven't you," asked her friends.

"Why, you know, I guess I have," she replied. She certainly had. When she perfected the melody that song "A Perfect Day" was published, and Carrie Jacobs Bond found to her surprise that she had touched the heart of the whole world.

Today, August 11th, is the anniversary of the birth of the beloved songwriter, who not long ago slipped away from this mortal world after she had lived more than four-score years of usefulness and left as a monument of that useful life music that stirs every heart and lingers like a benediction to remind us of her. Truly there could be no finer monument to Carrie Jacobs Bond than the songs she left behind her; timeless songs that carry the message of love and beauty down through the years.

Thanks for listenin' and good-bye, folks!

KATE SMITH SPEAKS —
TUESDAY, AUGUST 26TH, 1947

Hello, everybody! Now is the lovely time all over this nation, when that old American custom of holding State Fairs is flourishing in the warm August sunshine! Fairs in New England, in New York state, in Texas, Kansas, and Minnesota, just to name a few! They differ slightly according to the general location: down in Texarkana, Texas, for instance, they're getting ready for the Four States Fair and part of their festivities, of course, will be a rodeo, as well as the exhibits of beef and dairy cattle, chickens, flowers, hobby shows, etc. The Four States Fair at Hutchinson doesn't get under way until about the middle of September. Some of New England's fine fairs are over already, something to look back on with pleasure, but many are still coming up. And right now the Minnesota State Fair at Minneapolis is holding its 88th annual event, with all sorts of agricultural, cultural, and commercial exhibits. Whether the featured events are calf roping, bronco riding, and prize steers, or midget auto racing and maple sugarin' and square dancing, fairs are always a lot of fun.

It's the time when you forget all about work for a whole big exciting day, and pack the family off to the fair, off to see whether your jellies and jams, your quilts and embroideries, your cakes and your pies will win a prize, and to have a good gossip with friends and neighbors you've been too busy to see much of during the summer. As for the youngsters, their eyes shine at all the wonderful sights to see at the fair: the fabulous games, the enormous Ferris wheel that carries them up in the clouds! Sometimes I hear grown folks say with a sigh, "Fairs aren't what they used to be when I was a child!" Of course they're not! And when your mother or your grandmother was a child they weren't the same as when you were little either. Time was when youngsters went around with peppermint candies and apples on a stick. Time was when Eskimo pies and snowballs, flavored with bright-colored syrups, were the latest refreshment. Now it's double-decker ice cream cones. But the fairs haven't changed so very much after all, I guess.

They're still magic fairylands of music and fun and things to see and do, and if you can't turn back the clock and be a child again, the next best thing is to take a little girl or boy to the fair. Then, maybe once again, you'll catch their fever of amazement and excitement, and see all the sights through their enthusiastic eyes. And if you do, the scene will be gilded with star-dust and you'll have the best time ever!

And now, A MESSAGE FROM OUR SPONSOR...

(OPENING COMMERCIAL)

KATE SMITH:

I'm happy to report as summer's end approaches that there have been relatively few cases of infantile paralysis in the country this summer.

Delaware is a notable exception, since it has reported 74 cases.

The United States Public Health Service says there have been increases in 32 states during the week that ended August 16th, yet the total of 411 cases reported throughout the country during that week is less than one-fourth of the number of cases reported in a corresponding week in 1946.

Last year was the worst polio year since 1916 but unfortunately, less than one-fifth of the cases were paralytic, for some unknown reason.

As you may know, polio isn't always of the paralyzing variety.

Doctors know that every summer the hot weather will bring infantile paralysis, but they cannot predict where the disease will appear, or to what degree. But as I said in the beginning, there have been few cases this year and for that we should be thankful.

Now, Ted, what's new?

(NEWS)

KATE SMITH:
And in the new behind the news, sometimes I find out things the long way 'round…

TED COLLINS:
You mean the hard way, Kathryn!

KATE SMITH:
Well, I wouldn't exactly say that, because somehow or other, when some question is puzzling me, I'm sure to discover a little item that sets me straight. For instance, out in Seattle, Washington, I'm told, there's a night-blooming primrose which is rarely seen in the west and it blooms every evening in the garden of Mr. Frank B. Weber, of Seattle. And here I am, thousands of miles away from the Evergreen State, and I've been puzzling my brain over a little flower in my own garden that insists upon blooming only at evening, and now I know it's a night-blooming primrose! Mr. Weber says his night-blooming flowers are as accurate as a railroad watch—it begins to bloom promptly at 7:30 each night and produces from 16 to 32 blossoms by eight o'clock. In four weeks of blooming it produced 600 blossoms. Mine isn't as wonderful as all that, but it intrigues me because it sheds its beauty and fragrance long after my heavenly blue morning glories have closed their eyes tight and gone off to sleep!

And now, I'll be back in just a moment but first, OUR ANNOUNCER!

(CLOSING COMMERCIAL)

For countless generations, men in many parts of the world have followed the art of fashioning by hand from silver many beautiful and useful articles: beautifully designed bowls, graceful candlesticks, bracelets, rings—they're all objects that require great skill on the part of the craftsman.

But here in America, a young New York woman, Margaret Craver, is proving that there's plenty of room in the silversmith field for members of the so-called weaker sex. Right now, in Providence, Rhode Island, Miss Craver is attending the very first working conference for silversmiths ever held in the United States. She's really more than a guest at this meeting of those who make exquisite hand-wrought things of the precious metal, for she organized this conference herself. She is meeting with teachers from schools in all parts of the country in an effort to encourage more widespread creation of fine silver here in America. During the war, Miss Craver used her knowledge in physical therapy programs of various army, navy and air forces hospitals. Then, just last year, she was honored for her outstanding work. She was the only American, and the only WOMAN, invited to a London meeting of an organization of British silversmiths and goldsmiths. And the English, as you probably know, are among the world's most skilled workers in these crafts.

I speak of Miss Margaret Craver and silversmiths and their first conference today for several reasons: first, it's something that's happening NOW. Second, it seems to me important to discuss every now and then various ways of doing manual work, because there are so many disabled veterans confined to wheel chairs who are interested in hearing about the work of all kinds. Then, too, I always believe in giving credit where credit is due, and certainly Miss Craver deserves a great deal of credit for competing so successfully in what has long been considered a man's field.

You know, in this machine age, this plastic age, it's somewhat of a relief to realize that the art of working with your hands is not a lost art. The hollow-ware and other hand-wrought pieces turned out by Miss Craver and others will retain their beauty and originality for many years to come. They'll add to the tradition of the American taste for lovely things, for when you fashion something by hand, whether it be a patchwork quilt, a hooked rug, a crocheted bedspread, a painting, or a silver bowl, the beauty is something more than the size and shape, for into each hand-made thing, I think, we put a little of our love, our dreams, a little of our soul, and that's something no machine, however efficient, can ever give, for it lacks the golden personal threads to weave into the tapestry. Think of that, as you work with your hands. Be proud of your accomplishment as you fashion the articles of your own creation. It's a part of yourself you're giving to help beautify the world in which we live!

Thanks for listenin' and good-bye, folks!

KATE SMITH SPEAKS —
TUESDAY, JULY 13TH, 1948 (#3073)

This broadcast is on the CD. You can tell by listening how incensed Kate is over the possible effect of Communism on the minds of American children.

Hello, everybody! Well, I see once more, we women, or at least some of us, are to blame for something we would have managed to correct long ago if responsibility had been in our hands! (Laughing) You know, it's funny how just about everything that's wrong with our world is due to women. And sometimes, there is no argument about it, we are at fault! But when part of the blame for the housing shortage is being put on the shoulders of career girls, then all I can say is "How silly can you get?"

TED COLLINS:
Now, Kathryn, take the sensible view. Career girls in many cases no longer live with their families, even though they may live in the same town or city. They want their own apartment because they like to be independent, and this is taxing the short housing supply.

KATE SMITH:
Oh, so you agree with the Chicago Metropolitan Home Builders Association? That's exactly their opinion. They say they don't want to criticize career girls; they admire them greatly for their ability to earn their own way in the world. But then they go on to hand out a bit of advice; they say the career girl who for the present lives at home or with relatives is doing a really patriotic service, because when she does that, she frees precious living space for those who have no home at all. She makes room for young couples

just starting out in married life, for small families whose needs can be filled with a small apartment.

TED COLLINS:
There you are! You see the idea does make some sense.

KATE SMITH:
Yes, it makes sense. It makes sense like giving away your baby buggy and then having to carry your own baby in your arms! We're the richest nation in the world, we have thousands of square miles of open spaces, and then somebody comes out and says career girls are contributing to the housing shortage! Mr. Collins, I'm beginning to feel sorry for you men.

TED COLLINS:
I should have stayed in bed!

KATE SMITH:
And now, A MESSAGE FROM OUR SPONSOR!

(OPENING COMMERCIAL)

KATE SMITH:
And now, following up my argument about the merits of "women in the world today," I notice that in the Democratic convention, as in the Republican, women are playing a vital part.

Typical of these women representatives is Mrs. India Edwards, who is executive director of the Women's Division of the Democratic National Committee.

Mrs. Edwards had a few things to say to the delegates about high prices. And she said it in the best possible way, by emphasizing each point with an example which she pulled from a market bag she brought along.

Yes, the women are voicing their opinions at political conventions, expressing their willingness and demonstrating their ability to aid in matters of government. Which is just as it should be in a nation of the people, by the people, and for the people. Any comment, Mr. Collins?

TED COLLINS:

None whatever.

KATE SMITH:

Then, what's new?

(NEWS)

KATE SMITH:

And in the news behind the news, if you've ever found yourself in the middle of nowhere, with a flat tire and no jack, you'll like this item! Mrs. Mildred George found herself in such a predicament and she was determined that it wouldn't happen again. She started planning a gadget which would be the answer to that "get out and walk to the nearest telephone" business. She's invented a device called an auto-skate.

TED COLLINS:

Sounds pretty good...for a woman. What's it like?

KATE SMITH:

There you go! Pretty good "for a woman"! It is good, period. At least, it seems simple enough. It looks like an elongated roller skate, weighs eighteen pounds, and has six small wheels with a cradle in the middle. There's also a little detachable steel ramp. When you get a flat tire, all you have to do is put the ramp in front of the tire, attach the skate to the front of the ramp, drive on, detach the ramp. Then, just drive to the nearest gas station. It certainly does sound like the answer to a vexing problem.

Now, we'll be back in just a few moments but first, OUR ANNOUNCER!

(CLOSING COMMERCIAL)

KATE SMITH:

If, like so many liberal, easy-going Americans, you fail to get excited about Communism in our midst, perhaps you'll be interested in the latest exploits of the Soviets, which will, of course, in due time, become part of the organized plan to tear down the ideals of this Democracy.

Three leading Soviet journals have so far joined the new anti-religious campaign recently started in the USSR. They are the teachers' paper, the popular-scientific journal, and the organ of the Communist Youth League, all three bearing Russian names which I won't attempt to pronounce. The names are relatively unimportant. But the fact that these magazines have started a vigorous drive against all forms of religious belief certainly must give us pause for thought. Both Moscow and Kiev radio stations have started to broadcast anti-religious propaganda included in those journals, in addition to special anti-religious lectures. The most outspoken attack on religion made during the new campaign so far was in the Youth League paper which called upon the members of the Communist league to conduct, and I'm quoting now, "offensive anti-religious propaganda" by organizing lectures on scientific subjects dealing in particular with the origin of man and the universe. The paper admitted that there was still what they called a backward section among Soviet youth which has not yet overcome the prejudice of religion, and said that the League was therefore faced with the task of educating the non-party youth in an atheist spirit. "Religion" the paper said, "prevents people from being full-fledged builders of Communism, and conscious and active citizens of socialist society." There is more to this quotation, more along the same lines, but the important thing for us to remember is that the Communist Youth League members have been warned that they must not consider religion as a private affair and that any form of religious belief or "superstition," as they label them, are absolutely incompatible with League membership. All this, mind you, when an article of the Soviet Constitution guarantees "freedom of religion." However, it also guarantees "freedom of anti-religious propaganda" as well.

I mention this subject especially today because I'm thinking back over the last year or so, when in our own communities and in some of our schools, there have been attempts by some individuals to banish any form of religion, or prayers, or readings from the Holy Bible. Many of you may recall the attempt last Christmas to stop the singing of Christmas carols and hymns by school children.

Now, I am not saying that those who started these agitations are Communists, or being directed by Moscow. But I am saying this: this all-out fight against religion is a dangerous menace. A few active Communists in key positions in our schools or boards of education may succeed in spreading this idea among our own impressionable youth. So it's up to all of us to keep our eyes and our ears open, to watch the signs and be alert and ready to protest whenever we hear our word "freedom" misused and twisted about to mean not freedom or religious worship, but freedom of anti-religious propaganda in our midst. Don't be fooled! That is not freedom; it's an attempt at coercion. We must not let such things happen here, for this nation, its Constitution, and all of its ideals were founded on those simple words, "In God We Trust."

Thanks for listenin' and good-bye, folks!

KATE SMITH SPEAKS —
THURSDAY, NOVEMBER 4TH, 1949 (#3155)

Hello, everybody! Well, there'll be two more noses to be powdered in the 81st Congress, which is my way of saying that the Congressional election upset carried eight women into the House and one into the Senate.

TED COLLINS:
Yes, Kathryn, the ladies are to be congratulated for earning two additional places in the 81st Congress. Incidentally, the Democratic sweep apparently means that one veteran Congresswoman will again be known as Madam Chairman. I mean Democratic Representative Mary Norton of New Jersey.

KATE SMITH:
Mrs. Norton was first elected in 1924, and she's never been defeated. That's the highest praise we can offer of her record in serving her constituents.

TED COLLINS:
You know, Mrs. Norton's seniority will enable her to wield the gavel over the House of Administration Committee, if she wants the job. She has that right because she is the committee's ranking Democrat. She may pass this up, though, and try to reclaim the chairmanship of the Education and Labor Committee.

KATE SMITH:
Didn't she hold the Education and Labor Chairmanship for several years before the 1946 Republican Congressional sweep?

TED COLLINS:

Yes, she did. And whatever influential job she undertakes in the 81st Congress, we can be pretty sure she'll perform its duties well.

KATE SMITH:

Ted, I think that statement can be applied equally well to all the women who will serve our country in the 81st Congress. I know they'll do their jobs conscientiously and skillfully, doing credit to the citizens they represent and to women generally.

NOW, A MESSAGE FROM OUR SPONSOR!

(OPENING COMMERCIAL)

KATE SMITH:

Ted, did you know that for all their lack of kitchen conveniences, the American home-makers of a hundred years ago found life pretty simple, compared to the problems of home-makers nowadays? For instance, the New York State College of Agriculture at Ithaca submits this recipe of 1850, which I'm going to quote exactly: "To stir up a plain cake for the family supper, take the butter left over from breakfast, two or three eggs, a handful of sugar, as much milk as you think you'll need, and enough flour to make a thick batter." That's all there is to it!

TED COLLINS:

What, no salt? No baking powder? No flavoring?

KATE SMITH:

Apparently not! And I love that business about the butter left over from breakfast! The question in the minds of most of us might well be "what butter?" But butter wasn't a luxury then! If we really want to work up some sympathy for ourselves, consider those prices, as given in the current Ladies Home Journal. Fifty years ago, the Journal reveals, eggs cost 12 cents a dozen; leg of lamb, 9 cents a pound; Milk five cents a quart; and a whole frying chicken, 8 cents!

TED COLLINS:

But there wasn't enough money in the world to buy a package of frozen food, or a radio, or a television set, or a pair of nylon stockings!

KATE SMITH:

Why?

TED COLLINS:

Because they simply didn't exist!

KATE SMITH:

(laughing) I guess you've got something there.

AND NOW, TED, WHAT'S NEW?

(NEWS)

KATE SMITH:

And in the news behind the news, with Thanksgiving just around the corner, we have a late report on turkey production.

Agriculture Department officials now say that the decrease in production won't upset many plans for traditional holiday dinners.

In spite of the drop-off, homemakers will pay only a little more for their Thanksgiving birds this year than they did in 1947.

You may recall that I told you in an early forecast that prices on turkeys were expected to go sky high. Well, this prediction was revealed when the plentiful grain crop enabled farmers to fatten their turkeys cheaply.

So Agriculture Department officials estimate that more turkeys will be sold at holiday time this year. However, fewer are expected to go into cold storage, which means that we may not get turkey so often next year on hotel and restaurant menus. But it looks right now as if all of us will have all the turkey we want for our Thanksgiving dinner.

We'll be back in just a few moments but first, OUR ANNOUNCER!

KATE SMITH:

It isn't often on these programs, that I come right out and ask you who listen to do me a favor, but I'm going to ask you now to do just that. I'm going to ask you to do me a big, important favor; not because it will benefit me personally, but because it's my honest conviction that it will be for the greatest good of all of us, not only here in the United States, but in the entire world.

Regardless of how or for whom you voted last Tuesday, and whether your candidate won or lost, we all know now that in one of the greatest surprises of history, a surprise that could happen only in a Democracy, Mr. Harry Truman has been chosen by a majority of our citizens to guide the affairs of this nation for another four years. Never has a candidate been so counted out of the running before the people voted, and never did a President running for re-election get so little support or encouragement, even from his own Party, many of whom repudiated him and urged him to give up the fight. But he did not give up the fight, and America has given him his answer. The grave problems he faces in his new term of office are perhaps as great as any that have ever faced a President. And that is why I'm going to ask you that favor. Our country, our complete unity, is of more vital importance than party or politics. Our President, I am sure, will do a better job if we let him know he has our loyalty, our cooperation, and our support. So, I am asking each and every one of you to write him a letter or a card assuring him that now that a majority of the people have chosen him, ALL of us are with him all the way, in the interests of unity and peace.

Will you join with me today in writing such a letter to the President? It needn't be a long letter or a fancy letter; it may even be only a card. It's the message, and the spirit, that count. It might go something like this: "Dear Mr. President, This is to let you know that we, as Americans, stand solidly behind you in the tasks that lie ahead. We send our best wishes, and pledge our cooperation, in unity and good-will."

Will you join with me in sending such a message to President Harry Truman, Washington, D.C. now, today, so that millions of cards and letters will reach him promptly, inspiring him and spurring him on to successful conduct of the affairs of this nation? Please do! Let's forget party politics now and all work together, earnestly and energetically, standing united before the world, proving the strength and power of Democracy, the strength and power of unity, and the invincible spirit of these United States of America.

Write that letter today, will you? Thank you very much!

A novel idea, isn't it? Of course, Harry S. Truman didn't defeat Thomas E. Dewey by a landslide, so Kate's idea did have merit.

Thanks for listenin'...

KATE SMITH SPEAKS — THURSDAY, NOVEMBER 25TH, 1948 (#3169)

Hello, everybody! And a very happy day of Thanksgiving to each and every one of you!

TED COLLINS:
Yes, and that goes for me, too! May you all on this day eat too much and too long, forgetting diets and calories and the new look in waistlines! For this is the red-letter day on our calendar that comes only once a year!

KATE SMITH:
(Laughing) Now, Ted, don't encourage us to do any backsliding! Seriously, it's good to think that all over America church and other organizations, boys' clubs, Salvation Army, men's clubs, and other groups banded together in fine works are concentrating on this day on feeding the hungry and bringing cheer into the lives of others. Fun and feasting are in order, in the good old American tradition. On the fun side, it's football today for millions of fans in the stadiums across the land and for the small fry it's the parades that usher in the spirit of Christmas. The big parade here in New York City got under way earlier this morning, with thousands of youngsters and their parents cheering and shouting from the sidelines, and right now I don't even have to close my eyes to envision all you folks in the cities and towns of our far-flung map, especially you homemakers, bustling about putting the last-minute touches on dinner with a song singing itself in your heart because you're preparing to entertain those who are near and dear to you. Well, as I said a minute or so ago, have a real happy day!

NOW, A MESSAGE FROM OUR SPONSOR!

(OPENING COMMERCIAL)

KATE SMITH:
Ted, what do you know about carving the festive bird?

TED COLLINS:
I know one thing! Men who talk about the big one that got away aren't always referring to the elusive trout or bass! They're recalling an embarrassing moment when old Mr. Turkey wouldn't behave and slid right off the platter into the lap of the guest of honor! Believe me, I know!

KATE SMITH:
You and a lot of other male listeners, from all reports! Have you learned anything by experience, to pass along to your brother carvers?

TED COLLINS:
Oh, plenty. First you clear the decks, making sure glassware, china and knick-knacks are well out of the way.

KATE SMITH:
Then you wedge the turkey or chicken or whatever on the platter, don't you, Ted, so it won't slide around?

TED COLLINS:
Right, Kathryn! You can use a couple of carrots for wedges, or even chunks of bread. Have the turkey on a platter with the feet pointing at your right, grab the drumstick nearest you with a firm left hand, and with the good sharp carving knife in your right, cut straight down, close to the body, and twist a little to remove the leg, then it's an easy matter to cut the drumstick from the upper joint. Next you operate on the wing in a similar fashion, laying the pieces on a side plate, and you're ready to ask the folks whether it's to be light meat or dark, or a little of both. It's as easy as whittling, really, if you go at it with confidence, letting that old bird know you're the master!

KATE SMITH:
Sounds simple, Ted! What if the old bird SHOULD get away from you?

TED COLLINS:
From there in, it's anybody's job! Just smile nonchalantly, make a large and sweeping gesture to denote a generous host, and say grandly: "Just help yourself!"

KATE SMITH:
A lazy way out, if ever I heard one! But, let's get serious now and tell us, Ted, WHAT'S NEW?

(NEWS)

KATE SMITH:
And in the news behind the news, the kind of cranberries you're enjoying at your Thanksgiving dinner today may be out-dated on next year's menu.

Here's the reason: the Agriculture Department scientists who helped create the small-bird, big-meat turkey are working now to develop bigger and better cranberries.

These new berries were not available for today's dinner celebration because they're still in the experimental stage, but trials of the improved Thanksgiving treat have been made in four states in widely-separated parts of the country and if they live up to early expectations, they'll be given a name and put on the market for all of us to enjoy.

We'll be back in just a few moments but first, OUR ANNOUNCER!

(CLOSING COMMERCIAL)

And now, before this day of Thanksgiving is lost in time and memory, I would like to consider the blessings which are ours on this day!

There is much that is wrong with our world. Through the inventions of man, it is becoming smaller and smaller with instant communication and speedy transportation. A nation is no longer an island when those who dwell therein can forget that they are their brother's keeper. We have much to learn, and to forgive, and to understand in order that we may truly live as brothers and sisters, as sons and daughters of the one great nation which is humanity. But I know, too, that our blessings are many.

First of all, I am thankful for the peace that still, in the midst of difficulties, is balm to our hearts, thankful for our men and women on faraway shores who are endeavoring to keep that peace. I'm thankful for the plenty of the harvest; for the golden grain and purple grapes, for all the vast yield from the soil of America that is doing so much to feed a hungry world.

I am grateful, too, for the little, simple things about us; for the laughter of children, the flowers of springtime, the song of birds. For the grateful rain, the warming sun, the beauty of stars blossoming in a night sky. I am grateful for the fire on the hearth, the breathless beauty of snow on mountain-tops and the fragrant green of pine and cedar, thankful for beauty everywhere, and the power to see it, to feel it, and be touched by its magic.

I am thankful for the open doors of churches, for schools and long rows of books in libraries, for the great advances in medical science which fights disease and pain, bringing new hope to the afflicted.

But most of all, I am grateful, on this day, for the spirit, the will, and determination of mankind, faltering though it may be, to strive ever onward and upward in faith and hope, strong in our effort to build a better world to come, knowing that therein lies the promise of immortality, the lamp that lights the path ahead! And so, it is my earnest and fervent prayer that all mankind, everywhere, may grow in understanding, kindness, and human decency, in belief in God and the consideration of spiritual needs and may live in tranquility and peace, now and forever!

Have a happy day! Thanks for listenin'...

Your compiler selected key scripts to photocopy while he visited Kathryn at her retirement home in Raleigh, NC, on several occasions in the early 1980s.

KATE SMITH SPEAKS —
FRIDAY, DECEMBER 31ST, 1948 (#3195)

Hello, everybody! The nation's theme song today is "Ring out the old, ring in the new!" And you know, Ted we'd better talk fast this noon, because we won't be talking with our listeners again until next year!

TED COLLINS:
Which is just a hop, skip, and a jump away! If the single ladies want MY advice I suggest they get busy today, because it will be four long years before another leap year rolls around!

KATE SMITH:
(Laughing) Maybe the single ladies aren't as anxious as you'd have us believe to take on the responsibilities of married life, Ted. But we'll let you have your little joke. Tonight is the night when hearts are supposed to be light. Good cheer is in order, and parties, parades, and all sorts of festivities will mark the closing of the book for 1948 and the opening of a clean page marked 1949! At midnight in Times Square here in New York City, crowds of people will pack the sidewalks and streets, or maybe I should say the street, for Broadway is the street in this big town, darkness settles down over the towers of Manhattan, lights will sparkle, bells will ring, horns will blow, and the glad greeting, "Happy New Year" will be on every tongue. And while the noisy, carefree throngs are making merry, there will be crowds of other people to whom the contemplation of a New Year is a serious occasion; people who will go to their churches for the midnight masses and other religious services.

TED COLLINS:
Yes, and on the practical side of the picture, hundreds of hotels,

restaurants, night clubs, and theatres are wondering whether there's going to be a sizeable figure on the profit side of their ledgers. The past year has given Broadway a terrific beating and the night-spots are hoping to cash in on the New Year's Eve business to help them out of the red. Incidentally, what are your own plans for the evening, Kathryn?

KATE SMITH:
Me? Oh, I imagine my evening will be similar to that of many other Americans around this nation. I'm having a few friends drop in; we'll probably talk over Christmas, watch the television, and then just before midnight, we'll go to church. Now, that's the way I like to spend New Year's Eve. But I hope all you folks listening in, wherever you go, whatever you do, will have a grand time!

And now, A MESSAGE FROM OUR SPONSOR!

(OPENING COMMERCIAL)

KATE SMITH:
The fathers of America may have to pay extra this evening to have someone take care of their children during the New Year's celebration. And chances are, they'll have to drive the baby sitters home when the celebration is over.

These facts came to light in a cross-country survey by the United Press. And most baby sitters are upping their prices for the evening. Generally, the top price charged by the sitters will be one-dollar an hour, instead of the usual thirty-five or fifty cents.

In Washington, D.C., the New Year's Eve baby sitters have laid down some fine rules to go with their higher holiday prices. They insist that parents must get home at the hour promised and the sitters will do no household chores and they must have radio and television privileges. Incidentally, in the nation's capital, homes with television sets are getting priority rating on the baby sitters' lists, at least for tonight.

Well, television or no television, I hope that the baby sitters, the youngsters, and their parents will bring to us Americans, is higher postal rates on some items.

And speaking of "higher prices," one thing that 1949 will bring to us Americans is higher postal rates on some items.

At midnight tonight, postage will increase on practically everything except first-class mail and the penny postcard.

As far as the average post office customer is concerned, though, the biggest change will be an increase in Air Mail rates. Air Mail postage will go up from five to six cents an ounce on letters and small parcels weighing up to eight ounces. Heavier packages will continue subject to the Air Parcel Post zone rates that went into effect last September.

In addition, the post office is introducing a new air postcard that will cost four cents.

So don't forget, if you're sending letters by air after today, you'll need one penny more for each one.

Now, Ted, WHAT'S NEW?

(NEWS)

TED COLLINS:

And in the news behind the headlines, Kathryn, it gives me a great thrill to tell you, whether you know it or not, that once again by popular vote you are recognized as among the Ten First Ladies; not only of the nation, but the entire world! In the recent coast-to-coast survey taken by the American Institute of Public Opinion in answer to the question: "What woman living anywhere in the world do you most admire," your name was prominent among the first ten, and as a further tribute to the fact that you're America's most beloved personality, I might add that you were the only woman in the entertainment business to receive this honor.

And that isn't all! Once again, among the ten most admired women in the world, as decided by the almost four million readers of the Woman's Home Companion, we find your name. The qualities these readers like are courage, spirit and conviction, first of all. Certainly you have these qualities in large measure, plus many other lovable qualities that have won America's heart! Believe me, there's no news on the eve of New Year, that I'd rather report! I'm proud of you, and I congratulate you!

KATE SMITH:
Well, Ted, thank you! You quite overwhelm me with all these flattering remarks. I'm very grateful to the public who, after all, is responsible for bringing me these honors. I'll try to live up to them!

Now, we'll be back in just a few moments but first, OUR ANNOUNCER!

(CLOSING COMMERCIAL)

KATE SMITH:
On this eve of the New Year, whether we realize it or not, most of us in our subconscious minds are looking backward...

TED COLLINS:
Why, Kathryn, this should be the moment of looking forward! What's past is past, what's done is done. Man's best hopes on earth lie in the future, and when we think of the future, most of us, with natural impatience, visualize the immediate future.

KATE SMITH:
That's all very true, Ted, but we must look back in order to look forward. There must be a point of comparison, a balancing of the books. It is the general custom among radio people and writers to review the headlines of the old, lost year. But, as I've said many times before, each of us has his own headlines, his own secret, personal problems, his own private goals, and so, we walk back in our thoughts over the 1948 road to check our own accomplishments

and failures, measuring our contentment's and our blessings, along with our difficulties and shortcomings.

Most of us will search our hearts and minds asking ourselves what we do want, exactly, in the New Year? And I think we'll come up with an answer something like this: world peace, of course, but even closer in our thoughts, freedom from worry. We want, we Americans, a decent roof over the heads of our family, enough food to eat, enough clothing to wear. We want work enough to keep us occupied and to make an honest living, and we want, more than any other thing in the world, an assurance that our way of life, our opportunity and our freedom, will not be taken from us in this modern, stream-lined world leaning toward mass production, mass rule, mass security, mass thinking, mass propaganda. We yearn, in our hearts, to retain the individuality that made this country great and we see, in our world, more and more rules and restrictions, more and more limitations to initiative: burdensome taxes, high prices, less chance to save and plan for the future. We want the clouds swept away, and a chance once more to see the bright horizons of this golden land of opportunity.

TED COLLINS:
Kathryn, I think you're voicing the hopes and fears of millions of Americans with those thoughts. But while we carry the burden of a crippled world upon our shoulders, we must stagger along as best we can under an overwhelming load!

KATE SMITH:
Yes, that we must face. But our country has faced many tremendous problems and setbacks, and if we face these things together, determined to live and think and work in unity, we'll find our bright horizon and continue to enjoy the American way! Let that be our firm resolve for the New Year of 1949 and all the years to come!

TED COLLINS:
Right!

KATE SMITH:

And now, as is our custom at this season, Ted and I say a hearty thank-you to all you faithful, loyal listeners who through your friendship and kindness make these programs possible. To all of you, we are very grateful.

TED COLLINS:

Yes, that goes for me too!

KATE SMITH:

And now it's time for me to be on my way, so I'll just say Happy New Year, everybody! And thanks for listenin'...

KATE SMITH SPEAKS —
FRIDAY, MAY 6TH, 1949 (#3285)

Hello, everybody! Today, the light-hearted spotlight of the nation shines full on Louisville, Kentucky, where sports fans, horse lovers, photographers, newspaper men, and thousands of others on pleasure bent are already pouring into the city for America's greatest racing classic, the Kentucky Derby.

TED COLLINS:
Yes, tomorrow Churchill Downs will be packed with people from every strata of society. All the beauty and chivalry of Kentucky will be there, following the tradition that began on May 17th, 1875, when the first Kentucky Derby was held.

KATE SMITH:
They say it is one of the most colorful and exciting events of the year and I'd certainly like to see it. You know, it's a wonderful thing to think, not only of this great horse race which will draw people from every state in the Union to Louisville, but of all the other gay doings that are going on around the nation, now in springtime. Down in Memphis, Tennessee, folks are busy today getting ready for THEIR big show, the 18th annual Cotton Carnival, which gets underway tomorrow. Characters from comic strips will be honored at this year's Cotton Carnival and all next week there will be gay parades, fireworks, bands playing, and many other features which will celebrate and make merry! And now, before I forget it, I want to mention another celebration to be held right here in New York City, Ted.

I promised the Greater New York Chapter of the W.A.C. Veterans Association that I'd mention it in advance. Next Friday, one week from today, they're celebrating the seventh anniversary of the formation of the Women's Army Corps with a gala banquet-reunion at the Hotel Statler, and I hope they all have a grand time!

And now, a message from our sponsor!

(OPENING COMMERCIAL)

Now, Ted, what's new?

(NEWS)

KATE SMITH:
And in the news behind the news, for the next couple of weeks we're going to hear a lot of news about the Big Four as those statesmen meet in Paris. But this noon, I'd like to pass on some information about the Little Four. By the Little Four, I mean the quadruplets born two days ago to Mr. and Mrs. Charles Collins of the Bronx, New York. I'm happy to report that both the quads and their mother are doing fine.

TED COLLINS:
They're certainly keeping the hospital busy. More assistants are being added by the hour to take care of the two boys and two girls. Lebanon Hospital has already hired three special nurses to keep a constant watch over the newborn quadruplets, and an extra receptionist has been called in to help with the crowd clamoring to see the babies.

KATE SMITH:
And the proud father has had to hire an attorney to handle the flood of offers for the quads, offers which range from a completely furnished home to a television contract. I guess the babies and their two-and-one-half year-old brother, Stephen, are the only persons not excited over the latest addition to the Charles Collins family.

TED COLLINS:

You know, Kate, the hospital is going to provide all services free except those paid for by the parents' hospitalization insurance.

KATE SMITH:

Isn't that grand. But of course, it's just what we ought to expect. It's typically American, this desire to help the young parents in every possible way. Gifts and offers of assistance have been literally pouring in for the Collins family since the birth of the quadruplets was announced. Seems as if everyone in the country wants to congratulate the young parents and help guarantee a safe, comfortable future for the whole family. You know, an event like the birth of quadruplets makes any other news take a back seat. Folks just can't be bothered worrying about matters of national and international import when there's the future of four new Americans to consider. I want to join with thousands of other interested Americans in sending all good wishes to the Charles Collins' family, wishes for much health and happiness in the years ahead.

And now, a moment for a message!

(CLOSING COMMERCIAL)

KATE SMITH:

From the state of Indiana comes a big question for our listeners and us, Ted. It's a question that thousands of people all over this land are asking: do you think a person, sixty-one years of age, with ability, knowledge, good health and willingness to work, should be laughed at or ignored when applying for a job?

TED COLLINS:

The answer to that one, Kathryn, is certainly not, but unfortunately the facts are that most employers simply won't see, or interview, a man or woman who admits to sixty years or more. I don't know why, especially. Maybe the answer lies in the fact that many employers are getting on in years themselves, and they want youth around them. They have a fear of old age, and they don't want to be reminded of the passing years.

KATE SMITH:
Maybe you're right, Ted. But it didn't use to be that way. The world has changed considerably in the past half-century. When families were large and the womenfolk didn't have to go out into paying jobs, there was always plenty of work for grandma and grandpa. And if there wasn't, still they found a haven with their children, and knew the blessed feeling of being wanted, being useful. Now, with small families the rule and a man and his wife working, the entire outlook has been altered. Add to that the serious housing shortage and you have one of the answers as to why people today fear old age. It isn't that they fear gray hair or wrinkles. What they fear is not having any economic security, and I'm not speaking of a large group of men and women who feel they're too old, or too feeble to work, and who want or need the security of regular government checks to support them.

The group I'm thinking of is represented by just such able-bodied, alert-minded people as the writer of the letter whose question I quoted a moment ago. That writer has a college education, is well and healthy, ambitious and self-respecting. That writer wants not charity, or dole, or a life of ease, but simply the opportunity to earn a living, and surely there is something wrong with an economic system that does not provide that opportunity. Take a look at any of the want-ads in our papers today: ads that call for women not over 25, men not over 35! And yet many of the concerns which advertise for youth will complain about high taxes, some of which go to pay relief checks, and complain about the lack of energy and responsibility to be found in young employees on their payrolls.

In the name of humanity, in tribute to those who are not young in years, but are still willing and eager to earn their way, as well as for efficiency and experience, it seems to me industry might well make a closer study of this whole business of age. We talk a great deal about judging people on their ability and on their merits, but when it comes to handing out a job, the number of birthdays seems to supersede every other consideration. And so, I ask all employers now: Why not give the over-35s, the over-40s, yes, even the over-60s a chance? Why not take the trouble to check up in your own organization the record of the so-called "oldsters" against that of the younger groups on your payroll? The results might surprise you and might pave the way for a change of attitude and a greater respect for the men and women of mature years. Don't misunderstand me: I'm all for youth and giving youth a chance, but I'm first and foremost for people, young and old, and it seems to me they deserve an even break!

Thanks for listenin'...

KATE SMITH SPEAKS —
MONDAY, MAY 9TH, 1949 (#3286)

Hello, everybody! Well, there's a slim chance this noon that Congress may decide to wreck the White House and build a new and different executive mansion. A Senate House Conference Committee has been dead locked for some time on the question of repairing the old building, retaining its present walls, roof, and architectural character, or erecting a brand new structure.

TED COLLINS:
Of course, Kate, you have to remember that a repair job might be more expensive than a new building.

KATE SMITH:
So I've heard, but it would leave the White House with its outward appearance unchanged. And it would also preserve traditional aspects that a lot of folks would hate to see destroyed.

TED COLLINS:
On the other hand, a new building might last longer.

KATE SMITH:
Frankly, Ted, I'm on the side that favors repairing the present White House, and I think my attitude is typical of the average American citizen.

TED COLLINS:
I'm with you there, Kate. And I think I know why you favor keeping the present White House instead of building an entirely new one. It takes only a little imagination to picture the scenes that the White House has witnessed. For instance, the old kitchen, which later became a servants' dining room, has a big

plain old stone fireplace. It isn't the very best stone, but it's still in its original state and legends tell us that it came from a quarry owned by George Washington, himself.

KATE SMITH:

It would be a pity to destroy that, Ted. And think, too, of the room that once was Abraham Lincoln's office. A small bronze plaque on the mantel notes that it was in this very room that the 16th President signed the Emancipation Proclamation abolishing slavery in the United States. The walls of the study, just next door, have also witnessed historic scenes; conferences between Franklin Roosevelt and other World War II leaders who had great decisions to make.

TED COLLINS:

Kate, we're being completely sentimental about this problem, but then I think most Americans are when it comes to our historic landmarks. Folks have often described the President's mansion as the most beautiful building in the world.

KATE SMITH:

Well, it certainly is one of the most beautiful. And even if it weren't, I'd say let's keep it as it is. It's symbolic of the American way of life, a monument to the people of the United States and to our great leaders who have guided us wisely and well through years of freedom and Democracy. What if architects do estimate it will cost more than five-million dollars to restore it to its old-time grandeur and safety? Seems to me we manage to afford a lot of expensive items in operating our government. Well, I for one think the White House ought to be included.

And now, A MESSAGE FROM OUR SPONSOR!

(OPENING COMMERCIAL)

KATE SMITH:

A pretty New Orleans war bride is sitting alone by her telephone this noon, hoping and praying for a call from her husband.

Only yesterday she received a letter from him explaining his disappearance. He wrote that doctors had told him he was suffering from an advanced stage of tuberculosis and could not live more than one year. Rather than endanger her life as well and allow her to watch his suffering, he said he was leaving home.

His letter gave no hint of his destination nor of his plans for the future.

Mrs. Higgins had been paying a brief visit to a friend in Texas. She returned to New Orleans to find her husband gone. Her first thought was to check with his family to see if he had called to his former home or to his brother's home in an emergency, but neither the brother nor his parents knew of his whereabouts. Her in-laws could only tell her sadly that he had left on a trip out West. They said he wouldn't tell them any more than that.

Sorrowfully, the young war bride returned to her home. There, she found a large sum of money left for her support, but still no message, until the letter arrived.

Wherever he is, I hope that the former Merchant Marine radio operator will hear his young wife's plea and return to her. Perhaps doctors were mistaken in his case and his illness is not too far advanced for successful treatment.

Perhaps he will return when he hears these words from his wife. She says: "I don't know what to do. All I can do is pray he will come back to me. He needs me so much now."

Now, Ted, WHAT'S NEW?

(NEWS)

KATE SMITH:
And in the news behind the news, a fad for perfume-scented gloves may soon be sweeping the country. The first such pair, pink kid gloves smelling like roses, has just arrived in New York from

Paris and more will follow shortly in four delicious colors and aromas.

The perfume is put on the gloves in the tanning process and they can be re-perfumed after cleaning by using a glove-shaped blotting paper refill.

The other colors, all printed with a black lace pattern, will include white, blue, and chartreuse, and each will have a different scent.

I imagine that in practically no time at all, American glove makers will be using the same process on gloves and they'll be selling at a price that the average shopper can afford.

And now, a moment for a message!

(CLOSING COMMERCIAL)

KATE SMITH:

In cities and towns all over our country, in churches and parks and stadiums, native-born and naturalized Americans will gather on Sunday to give thanks for the blessings of freedom and democracy. Most large cities will hold special ceremonies in observance of "I Am An American Day." This annual celebration was originally conceived especially for those who had attained American citizenship within the preceding twelve months through naturalization proceedings. But " I Am An American Day" has come to be recognized also a day when the young people born in this land who have come of age, and older Americans as well, pause and pay tribute to our way of life.

Typical of the celebrations on Sunday will be the one staged in Detroit, Michigan, at the Belle Isle Music Grove. Four hundred youngsters in the motor car capital will present a pageant which they're calling "America for Americans."

Elsewhere in the United States, similar ceremonies will be held with millions of people rededicating themselves to the ideals and principles of our democracy. It is a thrilling and moving experience to participate in this rededication. Last spring in Central Park here in New York City, where our ceremonies are held, I stood among the crowds, and as many voices in unison pledged their allegiance to our flag, I saw an old woman with a shawl over her head. As she softly murmured the words, tears of emotion went sliding down her wrinkled face. Not far from her, a little boy, his dark eyes serious and steady, stood straight and proud as he, too, repeated the familiar words which suddenly seemed to take on new and deeper significance, and this small boy and the woman who shed tears of thankfulness and joy were only two of many thousands of people paying tribute to this land of their birth or their adoption.

Yes, Sunday, May 20th, should be a day of solemn thanksgiving to our land, a day when all of us who bear the noble title of Americans offer our thanks to God for his blessings upon our land and pray earnestly for his continuing guidance. There are those among us who seek to banish prayer and religion from our public ceremonies; there are those who say that religion and politics won't mix. But a vast majority of us Americans believe otherwise; we cling, and we intend to continue to cling, to our cherished slogan, "In God We Trust."

Kate proudly raised the flag every morning at the dock of her large boathouse at Camp Sunshine.

IV
THE KOREAN CONFLICT

1. MONDAY, JANUARY 2, 1950. Kate and Ted take a backward and forward look at mid-century.

2. THURSDAY, JANUARY 19, 1950. Kate praises women and speaks about the Horatio Alger stories of old. Ted editorializes against state-run gambling.

3. TUESDAY, FEBRUARY 7, 1950. Tokyo Rose is to be released on bail. Kate defends herself against an accusation of being a tool of Fascist interests.

4. FRIDAY, MARCH 31, 1950. The Federal Census begins tomorrow. Kate speaks of colored Easter chicks and of Passover.

5. TUESDAY, APRIL 25, 1950. Kate and Ted comment on western movies, old and new. Ted talks about the 5th anniversary of the United Nations. Kate speaks of the Soviets' change of heart since victory in Germany five years ago.

6. MONDAY, JULY 3, 1950. Information about the Red Cross locating servicemen and their families in Korea. Ted assures vets they'll not be drafted. The merits of summer camps.

7. TUESDAY, MAY 1, 1951. It's Kate's birthday, as well as the 20th anniversary of her start in radio. Kate condemns a communist May Day parade.

8. FRIDAY, JUNE 15, 1951. Kate speaks of emergency use of the telephone and of how to avoid polio. Although she doesn't know it, this is the last *Kate Smith Speaks* broadcast.

KATE SMITH SPEAKS —
MONDAY, JANUARY 2ND, 1950 (NO. 3456)

Hello, everybody! And a very happy New Year to you all! Maybe we're a day late in saying it, but it's never too late to give out with good wishes for happiness, and we do so now with all our hearts!

We've rung out the old and rung in the new, each according to our fashion. Now there's a brand new page on the brand new calendar, and most of us are enjoying a leisurely holiday today, which is doubtless very welcome after all the hilarity and the festivities of New Year's Eve.

TED COLLINS:
Which, here in New York at least, cost a pretty penny to the merrymakers, Kathryn. About a hundred dollars apiece, I'd say, for those who had dinner at an expensive restaurant, saw a Broadway hit show, and finished off at a popular night club.

KATE SMITH:
Maybe so, Ted, but the majority of people probably had a grand New Year's Eve on a whole lot less. Probably the people who had the most fun are just plain Mr. and Mrs. America, who went to a country-club dance, had a gathering of friends at home, or in the big cities mingled with the crowds on Broadway, or Michigan Boulevard, or Wilshire, or their own Main Street, blowing whistles or tooting horns, throwing confetti, and joining in the good-natured revelry to be found in all cities and towns when the bells ring, and the clock strikes twelve!

TED COLLINS:
Well, regardless of that brand-new calendar you spoke of a minute ago, Kathryn, do you know what I'm betting today?

KATE SMITH:
What, Ted?

TED COLLINS:
I'll bet many a check, and many a letter today, is dated January 2nd, 1949! Even if it is 1950!

KATE SMITH:
You're so right! All of us have made such mistakes in the past, and we'll probably go right on doing so, with each New Year.

AND NOW, A MESSAGE FROM OUR SPONSOR!

(OPENING COMMERCIAL)

KATE SMITH:
Like everyone else, Hollywood folks are looking backward this noon over the first half of our century. Naturally, moviemakers are thinking of the world's best pictures produced during that time. The United Press has interviewed six top artists to get the opinion of each one on the five best films of the past fifty years. I think most of us are interested in the selections of some of Hollywood's leading citizens, if only to compare their selections with our own personal choices.

TED COLLINS:
About the only thing they could agree upon was the decision that older movies were the best. Only two films from the past decade made the list. Those two movies are "How Green Was My Valley" and "The Best Years of Our Lives."

KATE SMITH:
Incidentally, we'd better identify the judges. They are Bette Davis, Donald Crisp, Samuel Goldwyn, King Vidor, and Cecil DeMille. We haven't time to name all their selections, but we'll try to cover some of the outstanding ones.

TED COLLINS:

Let's see...the film land celebrities spoke highly of Charlie Chaplin's "City Lights," Buster Keaton's movie "The Navigator," "The Birth of a Nation," "Snow White and the Seven Dwarfs," "Gone With The Wind," and "All Quiet On the Western Front."

KATE SMITH:

Another nomination for one of the five best movies of the first half of this century is "King of Kings." Incidentally, that one is still playing all over the world. A few foreign films were suggested by the movie land judges, but for the most part American-made movies won approval and I think that's as it should be.

AND NOW, TED, WHAT'S NEW?

(NEWS)

TED COLLINS:

The New Year 1950 is sleeping late this noon after a wild weekend. While we have a few minutes of peace and quiet let's size up that New Year and see what its prospects are.

One thing is sure. Old man 1949, his late lamented papa, was a cad and a bounder in more ways than one. But the old fellow had a lot of imagination, a sense of humor, and a gift for keeping out of serious trouble. Let's hope the boy takes after him in at least those three respects.

Looking around this noon it's easy to find a bewildering world confronting us.

Twin fears collaborate to undermine our confidence and make us reluctant to face the approaching future. The fear of Communism as a way of life, and the fear of Communist Russia as a military opponent, have made us doubtful of our prospects as individuals and as a nation.

Here at home, we find America in the predicament of a young man who has just inherited more money than he knows what to do with. Our earning power is still fantastically high as a nation and the economic prospects for 1950 are reasonably bright. Secretary of Commerce Sawyer predicts a prosperous business outlook for the coming year. Seventy-two percent of the companies surveyed say they expect sales to stay high at least for the first six months of the year. Some expect them to rise and most of them look for a healthy trend for the entire year.

Wages may go up slightly and our present wages will go farther. Lower prices have already been announced on automobiles, milk, soap, and other items. And reduced excise taxes, almost sure to come, will amount to price cuts on furs, jewelry, and luggage.

Food prices are expected to go down slightly. Rents may go up a bit and clothing prices will vary considerably.

Now, I do not mean to indicate that the inflationary cost of living is going suddenly down, but I do believe that there's a very good chance that the average American will find it a little easier to balance his own budget in 1950.

As for the Government budget, the prospect is not so bright. In spite of strong warnings, the administration apparently expects to keep on spending money on an enormous scale. At present we have a national debt of one-fourth of a trillion dollars, and that's a staggering figure.

The Government spent five billion dollars more than it took away from us this year, and many of us are getting sick of that.

On the political front Americans will find themselves torn in 1950 by the battle between the Liberals and Conservatives. The Liberals favor a strong central government and a more equal distribution of wealth among those in the lower half of the economic scale. The Conservatives are pledged to keep the country highly productive and thus able to provide the most things for the most people. Those of us who seek the middle course, and avoid the extremes, find the great battle raging within ourselves.

As for the conflict between East and West, the picture does not seem as dark as it was last year. We have won some victories in the cold war and they have made a hot war more remote. Our defeats have been severe, but not disastrous. The United Nations is a little stronger, and our best brains believe we can keep some sort of peace for many years to come. So, all things considered, I think we can look forward to a reasonably good 1950. Our problems are great, that's true, but always remember, we have the weapons for coping with them.

With confidence, courage and lots of common sense, I think we may be able to see the New Year through with quite a bit of decency and success.

And that at the moment is WHAT'S NEW!

KATE SMITH:

And in the news behind the news, while it is not news to most of us, I cannot let this first broadcast of the New Year pass without mentioning that it is Holy Year. To millions of Catholics throughout the world, this Holy Year of 1950 will be the guiding star of their religious life. For many of them, it will include a pilgrimage to the Eternal City of Rome, for six million pilgrims will journey to Rome from various parts of the world. In formally opening the Holy Year Jubilee on Christmas Eve, Pope Pius XII voiced the hopes not only of Catholics but of people of other faiths throughout the earth. "We expect the Holy Year," said His Holiness, "will see the return of international society to the plan mapped out by God." According to this plan, "all peoples, in peace and not in national selfishness, are meant to make up a great human family bent on the achievement of the common interest through mutual aid."

Now, a moment for a message!

(CLOSING COMMERCIAL)

KATE SMITH:
Ted, on this first day of the New Year, whether we realize it or not, most of us, in our sub-conscious minds, are looking backward...

TED COLLINS:
Why, this should be the moment for looking forward! What's past is past, what's done is done. Man's best hopes on earth lie in the future and when we think of the future, most of us, with natural impatience, visualize the immediate future.

KATE SMITH:
That's all very true, but we must look back in order to look forward. There must be a point of comparison, a balancing of the books. It is the general custom among radio people and writers to review the headlines of the old, lost year. But as I've said many times before, each of us has his own headlines, his own secret personal problems, his own private goals. And so, we walk back in our thoughts over the 1949 road to check our own accomplishments and failures, measuring our contentments and blessings along with our difficulties and shortcomings.

Most of us will search our hearts and our minds asking ourselves what we want, exactly, in the New Year, and I think we'll come up with an answer something like this: "world peace, of course," but even closer in our thoughts, let's admit it frankly, is the kind of peace which brings us freedom from worry. We want, we Americans, a decent roof over the heads of our family, enough food to eat, enough clothing to wear. We want work enough to keep us occupied, and to make an honest living, and we want, more than any other thing in the world, an assurance that our way of life and our freedom will not be taken from us. We are shaken by a sense of turmoil now. We sense danger in this modern, streamlined world leaning toward mass production, mass rule, mass security, mass thinking, mass propaganda. We yearn, in our hearts, to retain the individuality that made this country great and we see in our world more and more rules and restriction, more and more limitations to initiative: burdensome taxes, high prices, less chance to save and plan for the future. We want the clouds swept away and a chance once more to see the bright horizons of this golden land of opportunity.

TED COLLINS:
Kathryn, I think you're voicing the hopes and fears of millions of Americans with those thoughts. But while we carry the burden of a crippled world upon our shoulders, we must stagger along as best we can under an overwhelming load.

KATE SMITH:
Yes, that we must face. But our country has faced many tremendous problems and setbacks and if we face these things together, determined to live and work and think in unity, we'll find our bright horizon and continue to enjoy the American way! Let that be our firm resolve for the New Year of 1950 and all the years to come!

TED COLLINS:
Right!

KATE SMITH:
And now, as is our custom at this season, Ted and I say a hearty "THANK YOU" to all you faithful, loyal listeners of the MUTUAL BROADCASTING SYSTEM, who through your friendship and kindness make these programs possible. To all of you, we are very grateful!

TED COLLINS:
Yes, that goes for me, too.

KATE SMITH:
Thanks for listening, and good-bye, folks!

KATE SMITH SPEAKS —
THURSDAY, JANUARY 19TH, 1950 (NO. 3469)

Hello, everybody! Today I think American women may point with pride to their representation in the latest list of our nation's great names, *Who's Who In America*, and I'm not just referring to the face that there are 2,409 members of the so-called "weaker sex" named as outstanding personalities, nor that this comprises just about six per cent of all persons listed; a very high proportion if you consider how recently women have been accepted in our business world.

The truly hopeful thing about the list of outstanding persons is the number and variety of the fields in which women are mentioned. Nearly twenty-three percent are college presidents, deans, or outstanding educators. Almost as large a number are authors, artists, newswomen, and public officials. Club women are well represented, also. And too, you will find actresses, dancers, musicians, welfare workers, political workers, business women, librarians, religious workers, and many other categories in which women have become outstanding.

Of course, the listing I would like to see is homemaker, which would include housewife and mother. Naturally under our present business world setup, these unsung heroines of our country are never named in a limited list of outstanding personalities. We all know that they should be, and the percentage of women then would be suddenly high in any edition of *Who's Who* in our country.

But as always, the homemaker will remain in the background working with a will and without regard for reward. The only recognition she receives, and I might add the recognition most to be cherished, is her listing at the top of the "who's who" in the hearts of our loved ones.

TED COLLINS:
Now, a message from our sponsor!

(OPENING COMMERCIAL)

KATE SMITH:
Now, Ted, what's New?

(NEWS)

TED COLLINS:
A dangerous idea has been laid to rest in New York state, at least for the time being. We can well salute its passing. I refer to the proposal by Mayor William O'Dwyer that gambling on sports be legalized throughout the state. It is possible that other state governments may consider proposals along the same line. For that reason I'd like to take up the matter in some detail this noon.

In New York state, Governor Dewey answered the proposition with a prompt and accurate message to the legislature, and what he said on the subject of legalized gambling holds true for any state in the union. Governor Dewey declared bluntly that the proposal is shocking, immoral, and indecent. Those charges are easy to support with facts and good common sense.

First off, when any state legalizes betting on sports it says, in effect, "This state has no legal objection to your gambling on sports. We will supply you with convenient betting rooms, and the more you throw away on gambling the more money the state will earn for its activities. Go to it." Sounds a bit crude, doesn't it?

I do not think any member of this radio audience will disagree with me on one point—it is immoral for a state to suggest gambling as a fair substitute for producing an income by honest work. Nor do I think you will disagree on this point—it is indecent for a state to finance itself by exploiting the weaknesses of its people.

Don't fall for the fiction that a state will profit in the long run from open gambling. Montana, Florida, and Ohio have all tried it, and the results tell their own story. In all three states, the laws were changed. And in at least two cases, the states found that legalized gambling set off new waves of gang wars, murder, and corruption. It may be a coincidence; I don't know why even entire nations which have legalized gambling have found afterward that their finances have deteriorated and their people have sagged into poverty. It's the old "something for nothing" story, and it never stands up.

And there's more to it. If you legalize gambling on sports, where do you stop? Sooner or later somebody will propose legalizing other types of betting: roulette wheels, dice games, poker games, and the rest. So where do you draw the line? If sports betting is okay, why not the rest?

State gambling houses encourage men to squander time and money which should be devoted to their homes. The effect that open gambling might have on wives, mothers, and even children, is obvious, and a very distasteful thing to consider.

Finally, here is what I regard as the clinching argument. As most of you know, I have been an ardent sports fan for most of my life. I have always followed both amateur and professional sports with great interest. At present I am the owner of a professional team in New York. You will readily appreciate my deep concern on this question. Lest you accuse me of bias at this point, I'll quote directly from Governor Dewey's message:

"Gambling on professional sports events has been the most demoralizing and destructive influence in American sports." Then he continues, "The very idea of organized gambling sponsored by the state on events in which our sons and daughters participate is entirely abhorrent."

I agree on all counts.

In statewide gambling, huge amounts of money would be involved. Professional gamblers of the lowest order would be able to offer fantastic bribes to corrupt the young athletes of America. Frankly, such a prospect is sickening to any sincere lover of good sport.

The case is clear. There is no decent basis for legalizing statewide gambling. The solution is for law enforcement officers to crack down on illegal gambling wherever they find it, to punish offenders, and to remain vigilant.

If you like, you can base the case on this fundamental concept of American government. The state is established to promote the well-being of its people, not to undermine it. The job of the state is not to make bad living easy, but to make good living possible. I think American sport is an important part of that good living. I'm ready to take issue with anybody who wants to turn it.

That's what's new.

KATE SMITH:

And in the news behind the news, here in New York City at Bellevue Medical Center, a 29-year-old woman from far-off Boksburg, South Africa, is undergoing treatment for paralysis from the waist down. She is Daphne Ley, who broke her back eleven years ago diving into a swimming pool. Now, through funds provided by friends and neighbors, she is hopeful that the doctors here will help her. She was flown 8,100 miles to get this help.

Daphne says, "I am confident that doctors will be able to help me," and " I trust in the Lord because I know he can help me. I put my trust in him first, and then in medical science." With that simple, forthright statement, this cheerful and courageous young woman begins her battle to regain again the privilege of walking. The busy world beyond hospital doors moves on, and the headlines shriek their disconcerting news of strikes, murders, suicides, and disaster, but from that quiet hospital room comes the eternal message which mankind too often forgets, "I trust in the Lord and I know he will help me." Let's all of us hope and pray that this trust will restore Daphne Ley to health and strength.

And now, a moment for a message.

(CLOSING COMMERCIAL)

KATE SMITH:

Not many people know, or perhaps care, that this month of January marks the 115th anniversary of the birth of Horatio Alger. Yet for the generations of boys between the years 1870 to 1900, the Alger books were as popular as the so-called comics are among youth today.

I came across some of the Alger books last evening. They were the stories my grandfather used to read by the dozen when he was a lad. There were some 150 of them in the series, and every title was chosen to create sympathy, instill courage and ambition, or stress the value of honesty and hard work.

The Alger books were written way before my time, but there were still many of them around when I was a girl, with such titles as *Ragged Dick, Tattered Tom,* and *Luck and Pluck.* The tales were highly similar in formula: it was always the poor but honest hero who journeyed to the big city to seek fame and fortune, and somehow or other, he managed to distinguish himself by diligence and thrift, and gain success in a big way. The boys of the Alger books were always arriving home to pay off the mortgage, just as the cruel landlord was about to push the helpless old folks out into the snow. I suppose kids today would think them tiresome, even funny, if they could tear themselves away from the television or the radio long enough to read them. Yes, times change, and what was once considered exciting and interesting pales with all the knowledge and modern means of entertainment that youngsters enjoy today. But looking over these stories of another era, stories which stressed over and over again the value of honesty and industry, I can't help thinking of men like my granddad and other men of his time, and wonder just how much their lives were influenced for good by the Alger books and the primers and readers of the period. In the more than eighty years of his life, my grandfather stood for the fine American ideals of integrity, faith in God, hard work, and kindness to his fellow men that made him loved and admired by everybody who knew him. He, and those others like him, represent a way of life, a strength of character, which seems to be vanishing from the scene of this complex world of now.

Horatio Alger and his simple moral tales may not be widely remembered, but perhaps we need more like him, to capture the imagination and fire the ambition of youth. Anyhow, the boys of today, whatever books are their favorites, will not remember them any more fondly years hence than the boys now grown old recall the stories of *Luck and Pluck* and *Daring-Do*, which marked their childhood long ago.

Thanks for listening and goodbye, folks

At the desk with scripts following the switch to the Mutual Broadcasting System in 1947.

KATE SMITH SPEAKS — FRIDAY, JANUARY 20TH, 1950 (NO. 3470)

Hello, everybody! Do you believe that "charm" begins at 50? Well, the woman who has passed her fiftieth birthday may not win a beauty contest, but she is likely to have a poise that a 19-year-old beauty queen can envy but not emulate. A woman of fifty has time to develop her potentialities as never before. There is less fretting over trifles, more tranquility of spirit, more understanding. A mature personality is more bewitching in its own way than the mere physical attraction of youth.

Many women demonstrate that maturity increases one's effectiveness. Ethel Barrymore, Emily Post, and Mary Roberts Rinehart are outstanding examples. They had distinguished careers in the years well past fifty.

Qualities associated with youth are determined not by one's years, but by one's mental outlook. If middle-age tempts you to get into a rut, don't do it! Queen Victoria began to study Hindustani at the age of 80. Lady Mendl was just past 60 when she learned to swim. Adeline Reynolds graduated from college at 70, made her debut as an actress at 78, and became a star at 82. Now just how should the women of fifty accent her charm? It's easy. Don't try to look years younger than you are, or you'll only look ridiculous; stop apologizing for your age. Make the most of your assets gained by your practice in the art of living. Keep your mind alert. I think you'll find the years hang lightly when you continue to seek new experiences.

TED COLLINS:
Now, a message from out sponsor!

(OPENING COMMERCIAL)

KATE SMITH:
Now, Ted, what's new?

(NEWS)

KATE SMITH:
And in the news behind the news, to someone who has never owned a dog, the loss of a pet may appear a small matter, but it never is. Sometimes such a loss means real tragedy to the owners. I'd like to tell you a story today about Mr. and Mrs. R.F. Rummel of Long Beach, California. The Rummels have mortgaged their home, spent their savings, borrowed on a salary, and traveled eight-thousand miles through five states. They have done this in their search for their seven-year-old Boston Bull Terrier, which was lost four months ago.

The terrier, named Sissie, jumped out of the Rummels' car when they stopped for a moment during a trip across the Mojave Desert. They discovered the loss after five minutes, and retraced their route. By then the little dog had vanished completely. They think their pet may have been picked up by a motorist who saw it wandering along the road. Six cars passed theirs before they began the search. A service station attendant reported seeing a little black and white dog in a car that stopped at his establishment, but these clues proved worthless.

The Rummels are terribly worried about the welfare of their pet. Mrs. Rummel has made posters by hand to advertise the loss. Her husband writes letters to newspapers, radio stations, and humane societies seeking any information that may help them find their dog.

The folks in the desert area where the pet disappeared have also searched diligently. Oh, I wish I had a more complete description to pass on to you that might help in the hunt for the little pet. The loss is made doubly important by the fact that the dog needs treatment to prevent blindness. If only Sissie can be found in time, its sight may be saved.

And Mrs. Rummel, who is an invalid, will no longer suffer the very real sorrow that stems from the loss of a beloved pet. As I said at the beginning of this story, to someone who has never owned a dog, the loss of a pet might appear a small matter, but it never is to the owner.

TED COLLINS:
Now, a moment for a message.

(CLOSING COMMERCIAL)

KATE SMITH:
Tuesday afternoon I paid my first visit to New York's Coney Island in over five years. It was a beautiful day, and I just wanted to look at the ocean. You who have spent summers or winters or both by the ocean know these things, but you who live inland, do you know the spell of the sea? Do you know how it thunders and roars at the cliffs of Maine, how it splashes in a wild frenzy upon coasts of New Jersey, how it stretches and curls its white toes along the sand of Santa Cruz and Santa Barbara? Let us consider the sea for a moment.

The sea is the link between continents; it is American on one coast, English on another. It is American on still another coast, and Japanese beyond that. It is a plaything and a frolic for those who bathe in it; it is a living for fishermen; it is a challenge to sailors—sometimes friend, sometimes enemy. It sometimes gives the gift of life to someone ill, and sometimes snatches life away from someone hale and healthy. It always is both friend and foe; sometimes one is in the foreground, sometimes the other, but both are always there, lurking somewhere in its depths.

The sea is a thing of breathtaking beauty. It has a poetry at evening, a silken, lovely rhythm as the waves rise and fall in perfect syllables. There is a mist to it at evening, and sometimes there are slim wisps of fog that come slipping in from sea. At evening the surf is like pearls glimmering through the darkening blue, and the sand is the moving, shifting ghost of eras. The sand is the booty of the sea. The sands are bits of lost eras; they're crumbled Damascene blades; they're galleons that never reached Rome, and chalices and doubloons wrought centuries ago in ancient shops in Tyre. Yes, they're bits of lost eras, now but debris.

The sea is always poetry, always music. Sometimes it shouts and storms at the land, flings itself in a mighty rage and hurls forth again. Its poetry then is wild and frenzied, but it is a splendid wildness, and one you will remember always, once having seen it.

The sea is all things to all people. There are those who love it with abandon and joyousness; there are those who thrill to the taste of salt on their lips and whose hearts lift to a wind fresh from the salt and the sea. There are those who hate it and fear it, who hear only sorrow in its thunder and sighing and death in its story anger. And there are those who come, and leave, and come again, and never find the same mood twice, but always something different.

Yes, the sea is all things to all people, and yet, it is one thing to all: it is a force of God- magnificent, mighty and unforgettable. At least, I think it is.

Thanks for listening, and good-bye, folks.

KATE SMITH SPEAKS —
TUESDAY, FEBRUARY 7TH, 1950 (NO. 3482)

Hello, everybody! At least once each year it's my happy privilege to speak of one of the finest organizations in the whole world: The Boy Scouts of America. They are celebrating their fortieth anniversary this week, and the twelfth Scout Law, "A scout is reverent," will highlight the commemoration. Here in New York City, Boy Scouts of three faiths will dramatize this theme in exhibits at their exposition being held this coming Friday and Saturday. The Protestant committee on Scouting will have a booth depicting the "God and Country" theme. The Roman Catholic booth will feature a valuable church model, fitted with gold and ivory. The Manhattan Jewish Committee will have a booth displaying items of significance in the Jewish faith.

With more than two million Boy Scouts all over the United States participating in this anniversary celebration, it is a program of far-reaching value, and important to all Americans. In stressing this year a reverence for God and good, this fine organization is not only promoting unity among the people of all faiths here in our own land; it is also taking a step forward in promoting peace and understanding among the nations of the world.

TED COLLINS:
And now, a message from our sponsor!

KATE SMITH:
Now, Ted, what's new?

TED COLLINS:
(NEWS)

KATE SMITH:

And in the news behind the news, the attorney for Tokyo Rose is making arrangements this noon for her release on fifty-thousand dollars bail. Or rather, he is making arrangements to raise the fifty-thousand dollars for her bail pending the appeal of her treason conviction.

TED COLLINS:

I doubt if her lawyer will have much trouble, Kathryn. There are always enough individuals or bonding agencies that will be happy to risk their own dough even on a traitor to the United States.

KATE SMITH:

I'm afraid so, Ted. I had hoped that this would not happen. For after all, Tokyo Rose, or rather Mrs. Iva D'Aquino, has been convicted and sentenced to ten years for her treasonable war-time broadcasts from Japan. Her sentence also includes a ten-thousand dollar fine. Ted, wasn't bail denied originally?

TED COLLINS:

Yes, Kathryn, it was. Bail was first denied on grounds that the Government cannot extradite persons charged with treason. Therefore, the USA would be powerless to bring Mrs. D'Aquino back to this country if she should flee while out on bail.

KATE SMITH:

Does that possibility still exist, Ted?

TED COLLINS:

As far as I know, it does. So it looks like just a matter of time, about one week, for formalities to be completed toward the release of this convicted traitor on bail. Incidentally, Tokyo Rose's attorney says her fifty-thousand dollar bond will be furnished even if he has to put it up himself.

KATE SMITH:

I doubt if it will come to that. As you said, Ted, there's always some individual or bonding agency willing to back even those who have proved themselves enemies of our country.

TED COLLINS:
And now, a moment for a message!

(CLOSING COMMERCIAL)

KATE SMITH:
Folks, have you heard the Fulton Lewis program lately over this network? And did you hear a particular show, just last week?

TED COLLINS:
Kathryn, stop right there; don't say another word. I know the program you mean, the one in which Mr. Lewis mentioned a pressure group that has been trying to slander some of the most famous names in radio. This pressure group for which Mr. Lewis coined the nickname "Assassins Anonymous" apparently spends all its time victimizing well-known radio personalities. Its tactics are aimed at silencing the radio voices of a group of loyal and public spirited Americans.

KATE SMITH:
Ted, I'm quite familiar with these well-developed smear tactics. As Mr. Lewis pointed out, my name is included on the list of those being attacked by the pressure group.

TED COLLINS:
Yes, I know. You are accused of being, and here I'm quoting, "A dangerous and vicious tool of Fascists' interests." Your accusers also charge you with endangering the freedom of American citizens. Can you tie that! It's hitting a new all-time low in stupidity.

KATE SMITH:
Ted, I can only say that the "group's" accusation is too ridiculous even to be dignified by an answer.

TED COLLINS:
I agree with you there, Kathryn. However I know that you do

want to speak out against the shameful methods employed by that particular terror group and its fellow travelers.

KATE SMITH:

I certainly do.

TED COLLINS:

As Mr. Lewis points out, this organization of evildoers is trying to force off the air a few acknowledged patriotic commentators, one being Kate Smith. I hope you've noticed, too, that the underhanded scheme is not aimed at one network alone, but at leading commentators of various major networks. Furthermore, the smear tactics of the pressure group would do credit to the best trained propagandists of the late Herr Hitler or Comrade Stalin. Now, we have known about this deceitful scheme for some time, but until recently I hadn't realized how widespread it was. I still don't know the whole story, including the identity of the real backers of this un-American plot against leading radio commentators. I hope to know more soon.

KATE SMITH:

And when you do, Ted, I'm sure our listeners will be anxious to hear the truth about the group which seeks to destroy America with Fifth Column tactics. One thing is sure: even though I have been smeared by the Reds, I am not going to be silenced by any slanderous charges. My own conduct speaks louder than the venomous words of mud-slinging pressure organizations, and I'm still on the air.

Thanks for listening, and good-bye, folks!

At the table in Kate's large trophy room above the inside docks in the boathouse.

KATE SMITH SPEAKS — FRIDAY, MARCH 31ST, 1950 (#3520)

Hello, everybody! Well, as we all know, tomorrow is April 1st, but it's no April Fool's joke that the Federal Census begins tomorrow. As always, there's a chance that a few practical jokers may want to get in on the act.

TED COLLINS:
Any such pranksters may find that their joke backfires, Kathryn. Uncle Sam has sure and swift justice for anyone who impersonates a census taker. The penalty for impersonating a Federal Agent is one year in prison and a five-hundred-dollar fine.

KATE SMITH:
Real census takers will be readily indentified by official identification cards. Be sure to ask for such identification before you admit them to your home. There may be salesmen, solicitors, bill collectors, or just practical jokers who try to masquerade as enumerators for the U.S. Census Bureau.

TED COLLINS:
The doorbell ringing project shouldn't take long. It's expected to wind up in cities in two weeks, and rural areas in a month. After that, the facts will be tabulated for release to the public in readable form.

KATE SMITH:
Ted, there's been some controversy about some of the questions on the census form. Some folks feel that the question of income is too personal in nature.

TED COLLINS:

A lot of them can stop worrying on that score. The income query will be put to only every fiftieth person. And those who don't wish to answer the census taker in person can send their reply to the bureau on a special form supplied for that very purpose.

KATE SMITH:

On the other hand, all the information given a census taker is kept strictly confidential. Census takers must follow strict rules. They're supposed to count Americans, not entertain them. They're forbidden to talk politics, collect money for charity, or discuss any controversial subjects. The census takers' manual also forbids them to solicit subscriptions or to sell or advertise anything. In other words, the enumerating job is not to be combined with any other. Except in a few rare cases, I doubt if anyone will try to. If, however, an impostor should try to gain admittance to your home, notify the police or the FBI at once. They'll see that he doesn't try the trick again.

TED COLLINS:

Now, a message from our sponsor!

(OPENING COMMERCIAL)

KATE SMITH:

Ted, you know, I've never been a person to scoff very much at "flying saucer" stories. I'm frankly puzzled and a little concerned. But the newest tale of the "saucers" from Nashville, Tennessee, is almost automatically disqualified because of the source.

TED COLLINS:

You mean the two men who said they saw between six and twelve objects about five feet long flying overhead. I know the government gave its usual "no comment," but the men swore it was true.

KATE SMITH:

Ted, you missed the reason for taking this story with a grain of salt. Do you know what those men were doing at the time?

TED COLLINS:

Not partying?

KATE SMITH:

No.

TED COLLINS:

Or holding some type of supernatural session?

KATE SMITH:

No.

TED COLLINS:

Then, what could disqualify them as competent observers?

KATE SMITH:

It's simple, they were fishing. And their story of the saucers that got away is therefore "suspect."

TED COLLINS:

Kathryn, those men are responsible citizens. I don't think you should act as if fishing just naturally makes a man a teller of tall tales.

KATE SMITH:

In this particular case, perhaps not. But I'm telling you, Mr. Collins, anything a fisherman tells me of the one that got away, be it fish or "flying saucer" or treasure chest full of gold, almost has to be taken with a grain of salt.

Now, Ted, what's new?

(NEWS)

KATE SMITH:

And in the news behind the news, today an Ohio homemaker is collaborating with a New Jersey poultry farm to make Easter happier for thousands of American youngsters. Mrs. Aya Kiss of

Cleveland is credited with developing a chick that is colored before it leaves the shell, and the first batch of chicks tinted in this manner was hatched at Vineland, New Jersey, early this month.

TED COLLINS:
They were perfectly normal except for vividly-colored feathers, legs, and toes. Mrs. Kiss claims that the feathers will eventually assume their natural colors, but the legs will retain their rainbow hue.

KATE SMITH:
You know, Ted, this method of coloring chicks is an answer to the cruelty to animals complaint that arose a few years ago.

TED COLLINS:
It ought to be, since the coloring is injected into the egg before it is placed in an incubator. Moreover, an Agriculture Department expert says the new dye doesn't ever hurt the chick, and it makes them no less edible when they grow up to the cooking stage.

KATE SMITH:
Contrary to popular opinion, a lot of those colorful Easter chicks and ducklings do end up on dinner tables. I've heard of one organization out in Kansas City that takes care of unwanted chicks and ducklings after the Easter holidays are over. This group gathers up the fowl after the holidays and turns them over to an orphanage, and some mighty good chicken dinners are a direct result of the traditional Easter gift custom.

TED COLLINS:
Now, a moment for a message!

(CLOSING COMMERCIAL)

KATE SMITH:
At sundown tonight, Jewish families will begin observance of their happiest holiday. It is called "Passover," and in many ways,

it parallels America's celebration of the Fourth of July. You see, both occasions mark the birth of nations, and both are based on the ideals of religious freedom, equality, and justice for everyone.

Passover commemorates the escape of the Jews from Egypt after two hundred years of slavery. It is also an agricultural holiday, but primarily it is a festival of freedom. My Jewish friends have told me of the beautiful ceremonies that usher in this celebration. There are Seder dinners, as well as special prayers and ceremonies in synagogues.

The Seder is the highlight of the traditional Passover service. It is an occasion both serious and gay, and it includes every member of the family, from the oldest person to the youngest child. It is customarily held in the home, but many congregations and Jewish organizations also hold Seders for their elders.

The Seder is best described, I think, as a beautiful and impressive pageant which reenacts Jewish history. It reminds us of the eventful past, and offers hope for the future. As I have said, the Seder is an important part of the holiday that is the Jewish festival of freedom.

Just as that Festival resembles America's Independence Day, so does the proud Jewish heritage fit into America's cultural and historic background. I became more aware of this the other day when I learned of an experiment being conducted in Detroit, Michigan.

An organization there known at the Jewish Parents Institute is trying to recreate Jewish culture in terms of practical American living. The parents want to make their children good Americans as well as good Jews. To this end, they are teaching American and Jewish history side by side, to emphasize the similarity between their religious and national heritage.

One of the biggest institute contributions is a text telling the story of Passover in American terms. The text contains our national anthem as well as a Jewish song. In addition, the Institute has told the story of Passover on a recording, to an appropriate musical background. The entire project is one of which all American Jews should be justly proud. It reflects great credit on their religion and their country.

And so, as America's Jews begin their annual observance of Passover, I hope that news of this worthy experiment will add much to their happiness.

Thanks for listening, and good-bye, folks!

KATE SMITH SPEAKS —
TUESDAY, APRIL 25TH, 1950 (NO. 3537)

Hello, everybody! Ted, have you seen any old-time Western movies recently?

TED COLLINS:
No, Kathryn, I haven't. Even so, I can tell you that the plots of modern horse operas haven't changed, not since the days of Bronco Billy Anderson, who was the first movie cowboy. His first shot on celluloid occurred forty-three years ago, in an epic called *The Great Train Robbery*.

KATE SMITH:
The Great Train Robbery...wasn't that the first motion picture to tell a story?

TED COLLINS:
It was. And the man who invented cowboy pictures was a city slicker from Little Rock, Arkansas, who had never sat on a horse before, or so Bronco Billy claims. He came to New York to act on the stage, but he wound up on a horse instead.

KATE SMITH:
He had more than one role in that historic movie. He was one of the robbers as well as a deputy sheriff and a passenger on the train.

TED COLLINS:
And he isn't the only old time actor who had to double in brass for those early films. Incidentally, Bronco Billy is retired now after a career that included starring roles in four-hundred two-reel

Westerns. As I said, he claims that modern horse operas are no different from the earliest ones. They have the same formula.

KATE SMITH:

Just what is that formula?

TED COLLINS:

The ingredients are action, a light love interest, a sacrifice interest, and a bad man who does good deeds or vice versa.

KATE SMITH:

Of course, I think modern cowboy films are more grandiose than the first ones.

TED COLLINS:

Oh, sure. The producers throw five stagecoaches over a cliff now instead of just one. And they stampede five-hundred cattle instead of a mere one-hundred. Otherwise, there's very little difference between the first horse opera and the ones kids fall for today.

KATE SMITH:

And I, for one, don't see anything wrong with that. Some of America's soundest businesses are built on this same theory; when you find a good formula, stick to it.

TED COLLINS:

Now, a message from our sponsor!

(OPENING COMMERCIAL)

KATE SMITH:

A ten-year-old Pittsburgh boy is recovering this noon from serious burns because one of his playmates stuck by him after an accident. The hero is 13-year-old James Conners. The playmate whom he saved is 10-year-old Henry Leonhiser. Both were members of a group who used a light company sub-station as a playground.

TED COLLINS:

That gang of youngsters couldn't have chosen a worse place for their games. A light company sub-station is a dangerous recreation park. Henry is a lucky boy; very lucky to have escaped with his life after a foolish prank. His daring could easily have cost him his life.

KATE SMITH:

Fortunately, it didn't. Henry had climbed about twenty-feet up on a framework supporting high-tension cables when suddenly the daring young man lost his balance. Without thinking, he grabbed a high tension wire. The shock of eleven thousand volts hurled him to the ground in a burst of sparks and smoke.

TED COLLINS:

Henry's companions became panicky and ran from the scene. Jimmy Conners ran too, at first, but after a moment's hesitation he turned back, thinking that Henry might not have been killed.

KATE SMITH:

That action may well have saved the younger boy's life. Jimmy quickly beat out the sparks on his clothing and began to give artificial respiration. His Cub Scout training came back to him as he gave first aid to the badly injured boy. Jimmy kept it up until a police ambulance arrived to carry his friend to a hospital. Doctors say that Henry will recover, even though his burns are serious. Certainly his teenage chum deserves high praise for his quick action, but more important than this is the lesson that all the boys should have learned from the nearly fatal accident. Never, under any circumstances, make an electrical sub-station your playground. The minute you do, death may take it away.

Now, Ted, what's new?

TED COLLINS' NEWS:

Five years ago this noon, I sat before a microphone and brought you some of the most dramatic news bulletins of all time. I reported that American armies had met the Russians in flaming

Elbe in Germany. Adolf Hitler was cowering in a blockhouse in flaming Berlin. Mussolini was fleeing from the mob which was to hang him on a lamppost three days later. And in San Francisco, the leaders of nations had just sat down around a conference table. Their task was to write a charter to insure all nations against war.

This noon, on the fifth birthday of the United Nations, many Americans feel that this charter failed miserably. We're engaged in a cold war with Russia. It could develop into a conflict as horrible and costly as that which was nearing an end five years ago today.

There is no denying that the United Nations, whose gleaming new home is beginning to take shape here in New York City, is desperately ill. Any delegate will admit that. And the UN's Chief Physician, Secretary-General Trygve Lie, is traveling half-way around the world seeking an East-West agreement which could save it.

But it seems to me that in taking stock of the U.N.'s accomplishments, the picture is not as dark as some of the pessimists would have us believe. Whether you are hopeful or pessimistic about the future of the U.N., this noon depends pretty largely on what you expected at its beginning.

If you expected the U.N. to guarantee peace and world security, then it has certainly proved a failure. Four General Assemblies, three special sessions, and four hundred Security Council meetings have been held since that April day in 1945. And its pattern for peace looks just as shaky as did that of its predecessor when the League of Nations was blasted into eternity by the guns of World War II.

But I'd like to remind you that there is another point of view. Some of us expected the United Nations to do little more than provide a democratic forum for peaceful nations. Here, freedom-loving countries could at least turn the world spotlight on potential aggressors and brand the warmongers as guilty. In this respect, the U.N. is far from being a failure.

Actually, the United Nations was crippled from the first as the price of Russian participation. Moscow's insistence on the veto power should have been a clear indication of her intent to expand the Red Empire wherever possible. In the last five years, Mr. Stalin's hatchet men have repeatedly sabotaged plans for world security, and surely we can expect no guarantee of peace by the U.N. as long as one of its largest members is an active aggressor.

But let's remember this: in the long struggle of world peace, the democracies will not resort to fifth columns or lying propaganda of the dictators. Our greatest weapons will be preparedness and an enlightened world public opinion.

And if it does nothing else, the United Nations gives us a platform on which to stand and explain our case to the peoples of the world. Public opinion, both at home and abroad, is a powerful force in preventing war. We have learned also that it helps in winning wars.

Even a Kremlin-sabotaged United Nations can do one thing for this troubled world. It can provide a platform for the spotlight of public opinion. And as someone observed the other day, "A spotlight won't always stop a criminal, but it helps."

And that's what's new!

KATE SMITH:

And in the news behind the news, remember how the late President Roosevelt's little dog, Fala, appeared in so many of the photographs with his distinguished master? Well, it looks as though we'll soon be seeing President Truman with a canine companion. A little cocker spaniel puppy has been sent to the White House from San Pedro, California, as a pet for Mr. Truman. Dr. Richard Street, a San Pedro dentist, sent the dog as a result of a recent meeting with the President in Kansas City. Mr. Truman asked the doctor to send him a cocker pup if the dentist's dog "Taffy of Nevada" had a litter, so now one of Taffy's offspring has been dispatched to the nation's capital.

For twelve years I've had a taffy-colored cocker spaniel, as some of you folks know. I call him "Freckles" because his little white nose is plentifully sprinkled with brown freckles, and though I don't have a chance to mention him often, he's very dear to my heart. I know the President will become attached to his little cocker spaniel. They really make wonderful pets, as I'm sure all of you who own one will agree.

TED COLLINS:
And now, a moment for a message!

(CLOSING COMMERCIAL)

KATE SMITH:
As Ted told you a few minutes ago, It was exactly five years ago this noon that American and Russian armies met at the Elbe River after racing across a shattered and vanquished Nazi Germany.

It was a great day for the Allies and for the whole world. We saw that peace was near. We hoped that the fusing of brotherhood between East and West, symbolized by that meeting at the Elbe, would guarantee permanent peace.

At least it was a beginning, and a fine one. Two Russian officers present at the historic meeting were no less hopeful than the Americans. They expressed the wish that the meeting would be commemorated annually as a symbol of Russian-American friendship.

As they joined forces in the battle to free Europe, the Russians and Americans took an oath to do everything in their power to prevent future wars. I wish I could report to you this noon that both sides kept their promises.

But, we know better. We've all read the steadily darkening headlines within the past months. History has done what amounts to an about-face. This noon, eastern and western soldiers are lined-up again at border points, facing each other. There are no smiles today, just glares and bristling guns. The friendliness is gone.

But at least one of the six American soldiers who met the Russians at the Elbe five years ago still remembers his pledge. And this veteran, Joseph Polowsky of Chicago, has issued a plea for conciliation that I hope will be heeded.

Mr. Polowsky said, and these are his exact words, "The time has come for the nations to reaffirm that solemn oath of the Elbe. I therefore join in calling upon the nations for a new birth of conciliation and friendship, that the oath sworn on the blood-soaked historic ground at the Elbe River shall not have been taken in vain."

The Chicago veteran speaks wisely. We must not give up the search for peace, even though it seems far, far away in these troubled times. Only five years ago the Russians were our friends, and I can't help wondering if the Russian people themselves are responsible for the change of heart. If their leaders had not distorted the truth about America and our democratic way of life, we might still be good friends.

For this reason, we must not forget our program for peace. We must get the truth to the oppressed people of Europe, and the truth shall set them free.

Thanks for listening, and good-bye, folks!

KATE SMITH SPEAKS — MONDAY, JULY 3RD, 1950 (#3586)

Hello, everybody! It makes me very happy to report this noon that fair weather is in store for most of the country for the Fourth of July tomorrow. The head weatherman in Washington predicts average July temperatures from the Rockies eastward to the Atlantic coast, except for the upper Great Lakes region and the upper Mississippi Valley.

TED COLLINS:
Yes, and quite warm weather is forecast for the Pacific States and the western plateau area. In other words, typical July Fourth weather is in the offing.

KATE SMITH:
Only a few regions may find scattered thunder showers ruining their fireworks displays; and speaking of weather I've just heard about a leading meteorologist who doesn't think much of rain-making by the dry-ice process. He is Captain Howard Thomas Orville, who has just retired as Chief Navy Meteorologist.

TED COLLINS:
That doesn't surprise me. This experiment is still so new that you can't expect all scientists to agree on its usefulness. Mankind has been struggling against the elements for many generations. The cloud-seeding with dry-ice is a step forward, of course, but how big a step it's hard to say.

KATE SMITH:
Rainmaking or not, Captain Orville does have an interesting prediction for the future. He expects the day to come when man

will be able to forecast accurately the exact time that rain will fall in a specific area. And within the next five to ten years, he thinks it will even be possible to predict in advance the weather over the Atlantic Ocean. Yes, sooner than we think, mankind may do something about the weather besides talk about it.

(OPENING COMMERCIAL)

KATE SMITH:
Now, Ted, what's new?

(NEWS)

KATE SMITH:
And in the news behind the news, the Red Cross has reassuring news this noon for families who are worried about servicemen and their dependents in Korea. Red Cross chapters throughout the United States are prepared to handle inquires about the families of GIs either presumed to be in Korea or who are being evacuated from the war-torn country.

TED COLLINS:
Kate, I think this announcement needs a little more explanation. Earlier, the Red Cross had agreed to take inquiries about servicemen in Korea. This is an additional service to ease the minds of those who are worried about servicemen or their families presumed to be in that Asiatic country.

KATE SMITH:
This is a tremendous job the Red Cross is undertaking. Incidentally, the announcement does not mean that the Red Cross can handle routine inquiries about the location and welfare of any and all servicemen. It simply hasn't the facilities for such large-scale investigation.

TED COLLINS:
But if you're reasonably sure that a member of your family in the service is in Korea or awaiting evacuation from there, the Red

Cross will do its best to locate that relative and notify you of his welfare.

KATE SMITH:
Naturally, Red Cross chapters will continue to inform servicemen in the war area about emergencies confronting their families back home. The family has only to give the necessary messages to its local Red Cross chapter. And, of course, the agency will also relay servicemen's requests for reports about home crises.

TED COLLINS:
As for American civilians in Korea, their families here at home should direct any inquiries to the Division of Protective Services, Department of State, Washington, D.C. And questions about the safety of Korean nationals are being handled by the Korean Embassy in Washington.

KATE SMITH:
By the way, Ted, I've heard rumors about the possibility of former GIs being called back to service during the present crisis. Is there any truth to this?

TED COLLINS:
None at all, Kate, none at all. Scuttlebutt to the contrary, former servicemen cannot be called back unless they are members of the National Guard or the organized Reserve. That is official, straight from the Defense Department in Washington. Under the present law, these former servicemen can't even be drafted.

KATE SMITH:
Good. I'm glad you've cleared up that misunderstanding. Now, what about calling out the National Guard and the reserves? Is that action foreseen in the near future?

TED COLLINS:
My answer to that one is also no. The Defense Department says it has no present plans to call out either the Guard or the Reserves,

and it also says it has no plans to use the Draft Law, which has not been used since January of last year.

KATE SMITH:
Ted, I know these announcements are heartening news for all of us, and particularly for those who have dear ones in the organized Reserves of the National Guard. I pray to God that these men may remain on inactive duty and that we'll have no need for the draft.

(CLOSING COMMERCIAL)

KATE SMITH:
This is the time of year when the mothers of America give a great deal of thought to summer camps for children. "Shall I send my Johnny to camp this year? He wants to go," writes one mother, and she adds wistfully, "he's only ten and he's never been away from home alone before." Another mother writes practically the same thing about her little daughter, an only child, also aged ten.

TED COLLINS:
The trouble with most parents, mothers especially, is that they're not taking the viewpoint of the child's preference, but their own secret reluctance to part with their darling. That's a very natural feeling, of course, and I can sympathize with it. But I think summer camps are fine, generally. Most boys, and quite a few of the girls, too, are eager to go. Of course, it's important for parents to visit the camps in advance and make sure there are capable counselors, constant supervision, and sanitary living conditions. It's a good idea to talk over the camp with other parents whose children have been there during the previous summer.

KATE SMITH:
Of course, but I don't think parents have to be cautioned about looking into the matter thoroughly. Most of them are over-solicitous about their youngsters, and who can blame them? Those who run children's camps, incidentally, suggest that over-anxious mothers

and fathers are very apt to come around visiting their youngsters too often, and therefore the children don't have a chance to get over missing them. It's a wrench to part with the boys and girls who still seem like babies to a mother's heart. She can't help wondering, when night comes, whether they're getting to bed all right, whether they're homesick, whether they have enough covers, and all the little tender things a mother thinks about where her small ones are concerned. But a mother also realizes that a child, especially one who has no brothers or sisters, is often lonely at home. It's good for him to get with other children of his own age group; to romp and play, to learn to swim and sail, to take long hikes through the woods, and gather around a campfire for singing when evening comes. Youngsters adjust themselves easily to new conditions and surroundings. Camp life educates them not only in good healthy outdoor sports, hand-crafts, and woodcraft, but gives them excellent training in taking care of themselves and their belongings and learning to get along with people. Some youngsters who fail to pick up their things or make their beds at home are cheerful, even eager, about such requirements at camp. It gives them pride in accomplishment.

So, if your child wants to go to camp, and you can afford to send him, don't worry about how he'll get along. He'll have a wonderful summer, a brand new set of experiences, and he'll come home tan and healthy and will probably begin begging right away to go back to camp again next year. I hope the time will come when all children will be able to get away into the country for summer vacation. Children belong in the woods and the hills, with lakes and brooks for swimming holes, and plenty of space to play, and clean fresh air to breathe. It's part of their rightful heritage.

Thanks for listening, and good-bye, folks!

Is Kate making eyes at Ted?

KATE SMITH SPEAKS —
TUESDAY, MAY 1ST, 1951 (NO. 4000)

Hello, everybody! Well, there's a new picture on the old-fashioned calendars this morning. With April giving way to May parties in the park, Maypoles, and special festivals which have come down to us from the earliest times.

TED COLLINS:
Well, for you, Kate, it looks like the time of flowers, packages, and cards, to judge from all the things piled up here in the living room. Happy birthday, Kathryn, and many happy returns of this day.

KATE SMITH:
Thank you, Ted. Yes, it's birthday time for me and I'm knee-deep this morning in beautiful cards, letters, telegrams, and flowers; dozens and dozens of blossoms, many of them the lovely flowering varieties of daffodils, tulips, carnations, snapdragons, and sweet mignonette. Some of them remind me of the flowers that used to bloom in my grandmother's garden, which were always at their best around my birthday. It always seemed to me that there's no nicer time in all the year than May Day. It's a month of many meanings; the month of renewed spirit in the human heart, the month of promise for warm sun and lilies of the valley, and the month of emeralds. The emerald is the May birthstone, and legend has it that this green gem will sharpen the wit, confer riches on its owner, and lend powers of prediction. All you folks with birthdays in May, if you believe in the legend of the emerald, can just look into your birthstone and become wealthy and clairvoyant at the same time! (Laughing) So you see, if you were born in May, you're doing all right.

(OPENING COMMERCIAL)

(NEWS)

KATE SMITH:

And in the news behind the news, when you think of May Day in New York City, what does that bring to mind? Not, unfortunately, the pleasant conditions that used to make this date a day of rejoicing, for welcoming the arrival of warm weather.

No. May Day in New York City has a bitter taste because of a small group of "Hammer and Sickle" fanatics who take this occasion to pay annual tribute to their totalitarian chiefs, the International Revolutions in Moscow.

The Reds parade down Eighth Avenue, the "Left Wingers" trying to convince all of us that this is their day. Well, I have news for our home-grown Reds.

There's a parade today in the Bronx that may not get as much publicity, but it is a lot more important. Some five hundred real Americans, loyal and true Americans, are preparing to march into a large room in an office warehouse. There, this group of men and women will pay tribute to the brave men of our Armed Forces.

How will they pay tribute? Why, by donating blood to the Red Cross so that our fighting men in Korea will have a better chance for recovery from their war wounds.

This group of volunteers is made up of employees in A and P Food Stores in the Bronx. Their mass donation today to the Red Cross is expected to set a record for employees of any business organization in a single day.

And theirs is no one-time donation made only as a gesture to the day. For many of them, this will be their second blood donation since early February. To some of the donors, this contribution is a very personal thing. Two brothers, Anthony and Joseph Di Salvo, are giving for the second time out of gratitude for other blood donations that saved the life of their 19-year-old brother when he was wounded in Korea. James Whelan, another of today's blood donors, wants to help others survive this terrible war. His own 19-year-old brother died last week with a heroic group of Marines.

To all these patriotic men and women, May Day in New York has deep significance. Thanks to their parade, hundreds of American lives will be saved when American fighting men fall wounded on foreign battlefields.

Let the Reds and the Fellow Travelers line the sidewalks along Eighth Avenue here in New York. Let them take advantage of the democratic freedom that gives our enemies the right to demonstrate in our midst. But never let them forget, the loyalties of most Americans still belong to groups like that one up in the Bronx, to patriotic citizens whose thoughts on May Day and every day seek only to preserve and maintain justice and human dignity for a free world.

(CLOSING COMMERCIAL)

TED COLLINS:
And, now Kate, may I turn the tables? Suppose you tell us, what's new?

KATE SMITH:
Oh, no, Ted. That's your department.

TED COLLINS:
Well, then how about telling us what was new, say, about twenty years ago?

KATE SMITH:
Is this to be a memory test? Well, all right. Twenty years ago...that would make it the early thirties. Let me see. I remember...high churchmen were protesting the anti-religion persecution by the

Soviets. Some top Communists were arrested in New York and tried and sentenced. There were tornadoes in Texas, and there was talk of the Red influence in New York City Schools.

TED COLLINS:
I can hardly tell that news from the stories on my news wire this noon. Back in the early thirties, the Government was having gangster trouble, too. But instead of a Senate Committee to investigate the problem, the government boys were hunting down a bootlegger in the Senate office building.

KATE SMITH:
Yes, and here in New York the District Attorney's office was still reverberating with complaints about rackets and policemen were being suspended for graft. The Prince of Wales was visiting South America, the King of Siam visited North America, and New England was shaken by an earthquake. And that, at the moment, was what was new some twenty years ago. Satisfied, Mr. C?

TED COLLINS:
Not quite. Haven't you missed one event, one really important event?

KATE SMITH:
I don't think so. Maybe you'd better remind me.

TED COLLINS:
I never thought I'd have to remind you, Kate, that twenty years ago, Kate Smith launched a radio career. A career that was to take her to the top of the list as a singer of popular songs and to the depth of America's hearts as a person. Yes, Kate, this is your twentieth anniversary in radio. And like all your other fans all over America, I want to congratulate you on your countless achievements, both as an entertainer and a patriotic American.

KATE SMITH:
Why, thank you very much, Ted. You are so kind as always, and our listeners are, too. But this isn't just my anniversary, you know,

it's yours as well; the twentieth year of our association in this wonderful world of show business. I want to thank you for all you've done. And thanks, most of all, to the thousands and thousands of wonderful friends in out listening audience. Without you folks who listen, a 20th anniversary just isn't possible.

Thanks for listening, and remember: if you don't write, you're wrong! Good-bye folks!

KATE SMITH SPEAKS —
FRIDAY, JUNE 15TH, 1951

Hello, everybody!

My deepest sympathy goes out this noon to the parents of four young children who died in a fire in a six-room home at Everett, Washington. Those four youngsters ranging in age from two to five years might have lived if a person using a party line telephone had hung up when asked to do so by someone trying to phone in an alarm.

According to firemen and telephone company officials, an unidentified woman using the phone gave this reply when asked to relinquish the line: "Fire?" she questioned. "Who are you kidding? I'm paying for my phone, too."

The other woman had no choice but to hang up and try to reach help by another means. Only minutes were lost, but those minutes were precious ones. Firemen said a few minutes more might have given them time to attempt rescuing the children.

It's too late now to make up for that tragic error, but it's never too late to learn a lesson about "Party line telephone courtesy."

This is not the first case I've heard of where a home burned to the ground because no one could get a telephone line to sound the alarm. And in this particular case, it's especially tragic, because lives were lost—the lives of four tiny children.

I realize that some impatient callers will claim they need to make an emergency call when actually no emergency exists. We can't do much about that. But rather than risk serious consequences, as in the case of the Washington fire, it is better to give up the line when you're asked. The sort of conversation that goes on at great length can just as easily be continued after the emergency call has been put through, and I'm sure most of our listeners agree with me.

(OPENING COMMERCIAL)

(NEWS)

KATE SMITH:
And in the news behind the news, each year about this time, local chapters of the Polio Foundation issue the usual precautions against the crippling disease.

This year is no exception. The infantile paralysis season is beginning, with the warm summer months upon us, so the Greater New York Chapter of the Polio Foundation is distributing to school and college students one and one-half million cards listing precautions against infantile paralysis.

It's easy to obey every rule, and that obedience could easily mean the difference between good health and dangerous illness. First of all comes the warning to avoid fatigue. This means bypassing hard play, too much exercise, or especially difficult work.

Avoid becoming chilled. If you like to swim or bathe in cold water, don't stay in long, and don't sit around in wet clothes.

Avoid mouth or throat operations during any polio outbreak.

And don't use other people's dishes, tableware, towels, and the like.

Keep your children away from places where there is polio. Just where those places are, your doctor or local Health Department can probably tell you.

And if your youngsters are in a camp or playground with good health supervision, leave them there. Chances are the danger of polio in such cases is no greater than in your own town. Maybe the danger is even less.

But at the first symptoms of polio, put the patient to bed immediately and call a doctor.

Just as a reminder, those symptoms include headaches, sore throat and fever, an upset stomach, stiff neck or back, sore muscles, extreme fatigue, and difficulty in breathing or swallowing.

Of course, some of these symptoms may exist for other causes, but it doesn't pay to take chances. Quick treatment, if it is polio, often lessens complications. And take it from the Polio Foundation: at least half of all victims of this disease do recover without serious after-effects. If you obey all the warnings of the experts, you and your family may escape infantile paralysis completely, even if a serious outbreak occurs in your community.

(CLOSING COMMERCIAL)

"Kate Smith Speaks" will take the summer off for the first time since 1939, an indication of television's eroding of radio's importance and popularity. But what Kate doesn't know is that this would be the last "Kate Smith Speaks."

KATE SMITH:

Just the other day I found myself thinking of the story I'd heard once about an old gentleman who had worked at the same old job, for the same company, for sixty years. Finally, after three-score years of service, he decided to retire, and he talked, as people will, of how much he was going to enjoy doing nothing—and he certainly would never set foot in the office again. Two days later, there he was, back at the factory, "...just to look around and see how things were going." That's the way I'll probably be this summer, even though I haven't been at the job for sixty years.

Still, my life will seem very empty around about this time every day, because I'll miss these talks with you. Fourteen years, day in and day out, is a long time to be neighbors, yet for fourteen years you and I have met at mid-day to talk things over in a neighborly way. This association of ours has been far from a one-way proposition, you know. I have voiced my opinions over the air and you, in turn, have told me yours in countless letters, cards, even telegrams. Much as I love Lake Placid and the idea of having the entire day, every day, all summer long, for relaxation and rest, I'm still going to miss talking with you folks. I hope you'll miss me too.

In fourteen years you and I have been together at this time of day, we have shared many experiences. We've been through a lot together; happy times when we could joke about things, trying times when we prayed together. You have written me that sometimes my words have comforted and encouraged you, and I have often told you that your letters and cards, especially at Christmas, Easter, and my birthday have brought a great deal of joy to me. I can't thank you enough for all your kindness and thoughtfulness, and for the thousands of gifts with which you've expressed your kindness.

We'll be together in the fall, when we'll be able to share many more experiences together, but I couldn't let this whole summer go by without telling you how I feel. I hope you'll know now that I'll miss you this summer, and as far as the last fourteen years are concerned, I can only say a most heartfelt "Thanks for listening."

Two perfect squares. I was 36 and she was 64 on July 31, 1971, when we taped our second interview for club members at Camp Sunshine.

INDEX

Alabama Deep-Sea Fishing Rodeo – 186
Alger, Horatio – 242
American Red Cross – 268
"Battle Hymn of the Republic" – 102
Bond, Carrie Jacobs – 190
Boy Scouts of America – 249
Camp Sunshine – 30, 65
Cherry blossoms in D.C. – 23
Communist Youth League – 200
Craver, Margaret – 195
D-Day – 101
Dewey, Governor Thomas E. – 239
Dionne quintuplets – 51, 57
Edwards, Mrs. India – 198
"God Bless America" – 54
Hughes, General Alexander – 73
"I Am an American" Day – 226
Infantile paralysis – 193, 179
Lewis, Fulton, Jr. – 251
Luciano, Lucky – 165
Manhattan in wartime – 80, 217
May Day – 274
Mussolini, Benito – 135
Norton, Representative Mary – 35, 207

O'Brien, Margaret – 116
Odom, William – 189
Roosevelt, President F. D. – 120, 123
State fairs – 192
St. Patrick's Cathedral – 98
"Star Spangled Banner, The" – 19
Sullivan, Little Danny – 130
Talmey, Allene – 52
Tokyo Rose – 250
Truman, President Harry – 205
Twelfth Night – 116
United Nations – 263
V-J Day – 137
White House – 223
Wilkins, Sir Hubert – 26
Wives of presidents – 182
"You're Irish and You're Beautiful" – 89

Special Offer *from* BearManor Media

In order to properly appreciate what these scripts sounded like on the air, send in this coupon (or a copy of it) for a free CD of **KATE SMITH** shows aired on **June 7, 1944; March 15, 1946; August 28, 1946; August 6, 1947;** and **July 13, 1948.** Three of these scripts are in the book.

Mail the coupon to:
BearManor Media
P. O. Box 1129
Duncan, OK 73534-1129

Please send me the FREE KATE SMITH CD:

_____
Name

_____
Address

_____
Address

_____
City   State   Zip Code

Limit: One per household.

www.ingramcontent.com/pod-product-compliance
Lightning Source LLC
Chambersburg PA
CBHW060556230426
43670CB00011B/1841